overheard

conversations from the buses, boardrooms and bars of Britain

overheard

conversations from the buses, boardrooms and bars of Britain

MARK LOVE & JACQUI SAUNDERS

Collins

Collins
An imprint of HarperCollins Publishers
77-85 Fulham Palace Road
London
W6 8JB

www.collins.co.uk

1

Text © Mark Love and Jacqui Saunders 2008

The authors assert their moral right to be identified as the authors
of this work

A catalogue record for this book is available from the British Library

Isbn-13 9780007284276

Design and typeset by seagulls.net
Printed and bound in Great Britain by Clays Ltd, St Ives plc

Contents

Introduction

Neither of us is quite sure exactly when we each started making a note of other people's conversations, foibles and quips, but it began a long time before we met.

The decision to turn our little hobby into a book itself probably started with a conversation with friends. Someone probably laughed out loud or put their hands over their mouth in delighted shock, then said something along the lines of, 'You should write that down.'

So we did. We employed many techniques: eavesdropping, ear-wigging, a little lurking, nebbing, overhearing and snooping, to name but a few. Occasionally little nuggets have been passed down to us by conspiratorial friends who really should know better.

The result, we discovered, was a kind of kitchen sink snapshot of society caught resolutely off its guard, being real, being funny, occasionally sad – even terrifying. It spans every age, class and racial divide – a nation united in inanity.

It seems that the richest vault of human comedy and drama is around us all the time if we just stop, turn off our phones, MP3 players and laptops, and listen.

So why not just turn off, tune out and listen in? Who knows what you might be about to hear, and what you might do with it.

Mark Love & Jacqui Saunders
2008

Overheard something that you'd like to share? You can submit your own ear-wiggings at:

www.overheardconversations.com

PS Oh, just one more thing before we go... Just to make it very clear that the opinions and views expressed by the people in these conversations are absolutely NOT those of the authors or their publishers.

Acknowledgements

We'd just like to thank Jenny Parrot for recognising a good thing when she saw it, our agent, Isobel Dixon, for instantly 'getting it' and tirelessly championing our little book despite our enthusiastic hindrance, and Claire and everyone at HarperCollins.

We'd particularly like to thank all those lovely, lovely people – friends, family, care workers, Apple Mac computers (hint, hint), vintners and brewers of fine ales – who have helped us and supported us through the creation of this book (yes YOU!), and all those really, really unhelpful people who may be appearing in the next.

And of course it would be rude not to thank those unwitting, unaware and unidentified conversationalists without whom this would be an acknowledgement without anyone to acknowledge.

Toy Story

A town centre toy store, mid-December, and the manager and a Sales Assistant are staring intently at the stock on the shelves.

SALES ASSISTANT: Dunno what it is but Barbie's just not going this year.

MANAGER: Hmmmm... What if we put Superman on top of Barbie? Do you think that'll get her going?

SALES ASSISTANT: Nnnh, I don't know...

MANAGER: No! I know! Put Barbie on top of Superman. Yeah, that should get her going!

Zip It

A shop owner has been questioning her male assistant over a prolonged absence from work.

SHOP OWNER: So you're saying you were off for three weeks because you had an accident with your zip?

ASSISTANT: It's not funny! Little accidents can turn into something very nasty. I could have died. I was very ill, you ask Frank.

SHOP OWNER: You could have died? What actually happened?

ASSISTANT: I told you, I had an accident with my zip.

SHOP OWNER: Can you be a bit more precise? This is three weeks, not three days.

ASSISTANT: Look, I got it stuck in my zipper.

SHOP OWNER: You got your thing stuck in your zip and it took you three weeks to get over it? Marge had triplets and she was back at work six days later.

ASSISTANT: I got blood poisoning. I've only just got over it.

SHOP OWNER: How do you get blood poisoning from getting your thing caught in your zip?

ASSISTANT: I don't know! But I did! It was really serious at one point. I almost died.

SHOP OWNER: Well that would have meant for an interesting obituary, wouldn't it?

2

The Heroic Potato

A teacher has been leading a general studies lesson on genetic engineering. Kirsten, at the front of the class, folds her arms, purses her lips and shakes her head slowly.

KIRSTEN: I just don't think it's right messing 'bout with nature, miss. They should leave it alone.

TEACHER: Okay, but what about some of the positive effects of genetic engineering, like being able to grow disease-resistant crops?

KIRSTEN: I just don't want a carrot that's been messed 'bout with on my plate. It don't have to be perfect and all that...

HALEY: Yeah, it doesn't need to be straight.

TEACHER: Okay, has anyone here heard of the suicidal potato?

CLASS: The what?

TEACHER: Scientists have created a suicidal potato. Basically it recognises when it's become diseased and kills itself off to stop the disease spreading through the rest of the crop.

A wave of oohs and ahs.

KIRSTEN: Oh no, that's all right, miss! That's more heroic, innit? I'd be proud to have that on me plate.

The Speculators

On a commuter train travelling between West Croydon and Balham, a husband tries to read as he is talked at by his excited wife.

WIFE: Darling, you never listen to me about things like this but you have to listen this time! If property prices in Battersea are going through the roof then it's obvious that Balham will be next. Where I used to live, Blandfield Road; beautiful terraces, close to the tube, good school on your doorstep, Wandsworth Common just up the road...I'm telling you, if we bought a couple now we could make a killing! We've got to do this, Roger, it's one of those once-in-a-lifetime opportunities... And the real beauty of it is, nobody else knows about it!

HUSBAND: I think they do now, dear.

The Grieving Process

A young girl reacts to the news that mummy and daddy are splitting up.

ELLA: After Christmas, Mummy, can we get a new daddy? Joe was nice...

The Fablus Flautist

A couple fondly reminisce outside Ely Cathedral.

WOMAN: I mean, he was just a wizard on that flute.

MAN: Was he the bloke we saw at the Guild Hall?

WOMAN: No.

MAN: Oh, d'you mean the bloke at... You know, the one we saw at that theatre.

WOMAN: Noooo.

MAN: I know who you mean! That fella we saw at the outdoor concert.

WOMAN: That's him!

MAN: Oh yeah, he was *fablus*, wasn't he? Really *fablus*!

The Ear Complaint

A man visits his doctor with an ear complaint.

DOCTOR: Have you had this kind of trouble before?

MAN: No.

DOCTOR: Are you a wheezy type?

MAN: I have very mild asthma. Nothing serious.

DOCTOR: Right well, let's have look then. Good ear first....
Aha. And now the bad ear.

MAN: Ow!

DOCTOR: Oh yes, it seems quite inflamed. Does this hurt?

MAN: Ow, yes!

DOCTOR: Right. So have you been using a cotton bud in there
or anything?

MAN: No, nothing like that.

DOCTOR: Hmm. Matchstick?

MAN: No.

DOCTOR: Pencil? Pen?

MAN: I'm absolutely positive that I haven't put anything at all
in my ear.

DOCTOR: Well, it's worth asking. You wouldn't believe some of the things I encounter in this job. Tell you what, I'll make you out a prescription for some antibiotic ear drops. That should do the job... Knitting needle?

MAN: I'm sorry?

DOCTOR: You didn't use a knitting needle at all?

MAN: No, nothing at all.

DOCTOR: Okay then. Right, there you go. That's two drops, three times daily. Just sort of waggle it around gently with your finger to make sure it all gets in and come back if that doesn't do the trick, okay?

MAN: Thanks very much... I assure you I haven't put anything in my ear that I shouldn't have.

DOCTOR: Oh I believe you. It's just unusual that's all... You didn't have a swipe around with a bus ticket, then?

Yorkshire Watter

An elderly northern man is talking about his youth.

MAN: Me Dad were a miner, so he spent most of his working life down t'pit. But when he were topside, on a Sunday like, he fancied himself as a bit of an outdoors man. When it were fine he'd take us in t'countryside for some fresh air. Said it helped his cough like. Somehow he'd always make sure there were a stream for us to play in and he'd make a big thing about taking a drink out of it. He'd say, 'Lord there's nowt finer than Yorkshire watter.' He drank gallons of the stuff. Anyway, this one day he fancied walking a bit further, so after we'd built a dam and he'd had his usual drink, we toddled off upstream. Course we 'adn't gone far when we sees this bloody sheep in t'stream, didn't we? Swelled up like a bloody beach ball it were. Must have been dead for days. He weren't so keen ont'watter after that, I can tell thee.

You can't cheat yer Nan

A rather brash young woman is walking through a very select area of west London with her hounded-looking grandmother.

WOMAN: 'ow can yer cheat on yer Nan? It's not possible, yer mi Nan!

GRANDMOTHER: Shhh.

WOMAN: But how can yer do it? You can't. It's not possible to cheat on yer Nan!

GRANDMOTHER: Shhh.

WOMAN: I'm not using you. Yer me Nan! But yer shutting me out. It's like, cos I've decided I'm doing this, yer shutting me out and I've got to do it all on me own. Yer shutting me out!

GRANDMOTHER: Don't you think I'm entitled to shut you out after all what you've done?

WOMAN: But yer me Nan! I'd let you stay at my place any time you wanted. I'd let you eat me food, 'ave a bath, anything! Cos you're my Nan!

GRANDMOTHER: Shhhh.

WOMAN: *And* I moved out of your house to give you more room. That's what I did for you! And now yer shutting me out. I'm not cheating you. You can't cheat yer Nan!

Year Zero

A publisher stands before her assembled staff to deliver a rousing, morale-boosting speech.

PUBLISHER:...so I know we've had our problems. I know that the recent redundancies have caused insecurity, as has the speculation about the ownership of the title, but I want you...or rather I want us, to now put all that behind us and concentrate on building a future for ourselves and the magazine. Today is year zero. Nothing that happened before today matters. All disputes are forgiven and forgotten. Clear slates all around and that includes the naysayers too.
I want a better attitude, a more positive attitude. No more grumbling in corners. If you've got something to say, you can come and say it to me direct, I won't hold it against you. Remember – year zero, all right? Okay, let's go to lunch.

SUB-EDITOR: (quietly) Er, wasn't year zero the process of systematic slaughter of innocent people by an insane dictator?

STAFF WRITER: Yup. Business as usual then.

The Dry-Cleaner

A woman in a dry-cleaner's shop pulls a coat out of a bag.

WOMAN: I'd like to have this cleaned, please.

DRY-CLEANER: Right, that'll be... What's that?

WOMAN: It's a coat, a man's coat.

DRY-CLEANER: What's that on it?

WOMAN: What?

DRY-CLEANER: (pointing) *There*.

WOMAN: Oh, I expect it's a cat hair, I caught the cat sleeping on it.

DRY-CLEANER: Well I can't accept that, I'm afraid.

WOMAN: I beg your pardon?

DRY-CLEANER: I'm not touching it. I have an allergy.

WOMAN: It's just a cat hair.

DRY-CLEANER: I'm sorry but I can't accept it. If you take it away and remove any cat hair I'll be pleased to clean it.

WOMAN: You mean take it away and clean it? Don't you think I brought it to you because I wanted it cleaned?

DRY-CLEANER: I can't take it, sorry.

WOMAN: This is ridiculous! You must have dozens of things brought in every day that have cat hairs on them! You seriously expect me to take this home, clean it, and then bring it back for you to clean it again?

DRY-CLEANER: Sorry. I've got an allergy.

WOMAN: (furious) Has it ever occurred to you that you might have gone into the wrong profession?

She exits in a swirl of loose cat hair.

Note: The dry-cleaners went out of business two weeks later.

The Crunch

An announcement at a south London railway station.

ANNOUNCER: Passengers awaiting the next Victoria train...
Ladies and gentlemen, you're going to love this one. Well,
you're not, but anyway... The reason your next Victoria-bound
train is running late, ladies and gentlemen, is apparently due
to there being a crisp packet on the line at Carshalton
Beeches. Imagine that, eh? Gord knows how many tons of
brand-new passenger train brought to a standstill by a crisp
packet. Just think, ladies and gentlemen, if the Kuwaitis had
scattered a couple of dozen Golden Wonder packets in front of
Saddam's tanks, the war might never have 'appened.

Would You?

An indignant sixth-former holds forth on that year's notorious New Year's party, which took place at her house.

GIRL 1: And you'll never guess what happened.

GIRL 2: Oh, is this about M and A?

GIRL 1: Yeah, I mean, did you hear? On *my* bed. I don't think that's right, do you? That's minging. Dan? Dan, if you were at someone's party would you do it on their bed?

DAN: What?

GIRL 2: You know – *do it*. On someone's bed?

DAN: Hhhmm.

GIRL 1: I mean, that's bad enough. But she said to me, 'Oh we did it *on* your bed, not in your bed.' Like that's supposed to make it all right! Not *in* my bed but *on* it! I mean, like, urghh! I mean, would you have done it on *my* bed, Dan?

Dan considers this very carefully.

DAN: No, I don't think I'd have done it *on* your bed. I think I'd probably have done it on your floor. Next to your bed but not *on* your bed.

Girl 1 and Girl 2 regard Dan incredulously.

DAN: What?

Girl 1 and Girl 2 tut.

DAN: You know, I'm surprised someone hasn't warned him about that girl.

The Communication Age

A son, who has just arrived home from work, answers the phone.

MOTHER: Hello, love, it's me.

SON: Hi, Mum. How you doing?

MOTHER: Oh, I've got you at last, have I? You wouldn't believe the problems I've had.

SON: Why?

MOTHER: Well, every time I phoned you I was getting through to this old woman.

SON: You mean you misdialled.

MOTHER: No, I don't know what it was. Our Rachel had to call t'phone company for me. I'm telling you, every time I tried to call your number I got this old woman. Ooh, she were bad-tempered. 'Stop calling me,' she says. 'I'm not your bloody son.' Right rude she were.

SON: It was probably a computer glitch at their end, Mum.

MOTHER: Yes, but why did it happen to me?

SON: Well, it's nothing personal, Mum, it was probably just a typing error.

MOTHER: But why should it just affect me? Things are always happening to me.

SON: Honest, Mum, it's nothing to do with you personally.

MOTHER: Yes it is! It's me who has to say sorry!

SON: I mean, it wasn't someone getting at you on purpose! It was just an accident.

MOTHER: But *you* haven't had any problems, have you?

SON: I'm not with your company, Mum.

MOTHER: Well why would it just be them?

SON: Mum! I don't know! It was probably the little man who connects the phones put the wrong two wires together.

MOTHER: Well it could happen again!

SON: It probably won't, Mum.

MOTHER: Oooh, I don't know. Things are always happening to me. Anyway, love, I won't keep you...

SON: Mum, wait a minute, what were you phoning for in the first place?

MOTHER: Eh?

SON: What were you phoning for?

MOTHER: To find out if I could get through!

SON: No, I mean before you found out there was a problem.

MOTHER: Oooh, I don't know. It's all confused me a bit.

SON: You and me both, Mum. You and me both.

The School Trip

The leader of a recent skiing trip addresses the staff briefing meeting on Monday morning.

PE TEACHER: Morning. I'd just like to thank all the members of staff who helped out on the ski trip. Particularly Steve and Marilyn who drove the mini-buses and picked everyone up at 5 a.m. The kids were brilliant! Really well-behaved and they had a great time. There was, er, just the one minor trip to the police station...

DEPUTY HEAD: Marilyn!

MARILYN: Sorreee! It's *alright*. I got off!

The Comedic Properties of Fruit

A team of experienced and not-so-experienced comedy writers are assembled to discuss the latest material submitted for a popular TV sketch show. A heated discussion has taken place for some thirty minutes on whether an apple can ever be funny.

OLDER WRITER: Look, all I'm saying is that if the camera pulls away to reveal that he has got a sausage stuck up his arse, *that* is funny. If he's got an apple stuck up his arse, it isn't. Simple as that.

PRODUCER: Well, I can see your point, but isn't an apple just a bit amusing? I mean, we all laughed.

OLDER WRITER: Yes, well, we're professionals...

YOUNGER WRITER: Oh for god's sake!

OLDER WRITER: No, listen. I've been in this game...

YOUNGER WRITER: Man and boy.

OLDER WRITER: ...man and boy nigh on fifteen years and I can tell you that I've never, ever got a laugh out of a piece of fruit.

PRODUCER: Oh come on, bananas are funny.

OLDER WRITER: Not really fruit though, are they?

YOUNGER WRITER: Er, *yes*.

PRODUCER: Look, can't we all just agree that the camera should pull back and reveal that he has something that is amusing, be it fruit or animal derivative, sticking out of his arse?

FEMALE WRITER: Forgive me for pointing this out, but won't a sausage look a bit like a turd?

PRODUCER: Oh, now there's a point!

OLDER WRITER: Look, if it was a crab apple, I can see how that would be funny.

YOUNGER WRITER: How would the viewer know it was a sodding crab apple?

PRODUCER: Look, let's leave that one and move on to the wine expert sketch. Basically what happens is we set up the idea that our celebrity wine expert has a new tasting programme on TV. Roll credits, opening shot shows our celebrity wine expert lookalike gobbing off the stage manager. There's puffing, panting and groaning, then our wine expert wipes her mouth and to camera says, 'Hmm, I'm getting ripe berries, sunkissed privet hedge, bus stops...' Blah, blah, blah. Any thoughts?

OLDER WRITER: Look, how many more bloody times? Berries, apples, any kind of bloody fruit. They're just *not* funny, all right?

Winsor

A railway employee is approached by a Russian passenger at Victoria Station ticket barrier.

PASSENGER: (pointing at the London Bridge train) Excuse me pliz. Winsor?

RAILWAY EMPLOYEE: No sir, you need to take that train there, sir. Change at Clapham Junction.

PASSENGER: No! Winsor!

RAILWAY EMPLOYEE: Yes, sir, that train over there. You'll need to change at Clapham Junction for the train to Windsor, which will depart from platform eleven.

PASSENGER: (irate) NO! WIN-SOR!

Pause.

RAILWAY EMPLOYEE: Yes, sir, I understand. You take the train there, the one waiting on platform eleven and you change at Clapham Junction, which will be the next stop...

PASSENGER: (very irate) NO! NO! NO! I vant *WIN-SOR*.

RAILWAY EMPLOYEE: (pointing to London Bridge train) That one, mate.

PASSENGER: (delighted) Senk you!

RAILWAY EMPLOYEE: My pleasure, sir.

The Chocolate Teapot

An exhausted-looking wife is chatting to her neighbour, watching as her husband and the removal men load their furniture into the removal lorry. Her face reflects her anger.

WIFE: Yes, well, we would have been gone about two hours ago, if it wasn't for sonny Jim over there. Can you imagine, I spend days going round the packed boxes and furniture, marking them with coloured stickers so the removal men will know which rooms the boxes need to be left in at the new place. Then, along comes my darling husband an hour before the removal company arrives, with a handful of coloured stickers that he's assumed the kids stuck on the boxes and furniture and has spent the best part of an hour finding and removing. Oooh, if a divorce was cheaper than moving then he'd be gone!

Why?

A father and his young son are travelling on the Central Line. The father reads a book on parenting, while the little boy clambers around restlessly.

BOY: Daddy?

FATHER: (not looking up) Hmm?

BOY: Why does the train go underground?

FATHER: Because it's easier to travel across London when you're underground.

BOY: Why?

FATHER: Because then you don't get stuck in traffic jams.

BOY: Why?

FATHER: Because there are no cars underground.

BOY: Why?

FATHER: Because cars travel on roads above the ground.

BOY: Why?

FATHER: Because that's what they were designed to do.

BOY: Why?

FATHER: (sighing) Because people needed to get around faster.

BOY: (pauses, considering this) Daddy?

FATHER: What?

BOY: If they designed cars to get around faster, then why do we have to travel on the underground?

FATHER: Oh, just because!

Reclassifying the Kids

Two mums, both mothers of mixed-race children stand, at the school gates, arms crossed indignantly.

MUM 1: So she says I can't call 'em that no more...

MUM 2: No!

MUM 1: I says, wot? She says Indian. Well, wot am I supposed to call 'em? She says cahncil says you gotta call 'em...

MUM 2: Bengali British. Yeah, I know!

MUM 1: Well! I mean, I remember when they wuz jus' black!

MUM 2: Yeah. Then it were Black British!

MUM 1: After that it wuz mixed-race...

MUM 2: Yeah.

MUM 1: I mean why's it any of their fackin' business anyway?

MUM 2: Wrinkles her nose and shakes her head.

MUM 1: I mean, you ain't bovvered, is ya?

MUM 2: Nah.

MUM 1: Well then!

The Art of Luvvy

A comedy actor at a celebrity wedding is talking about 'luvvydom'.

ACTOR: We kissed, reminisced and hugged for about an hour before we both had the nerve to admit we didn't know who the fuck the other was.

Wolves

A beautiful summer's day. The owners of toy spaniels are chatting in the park, their dogs – in winter coats – shivering in their arms.

COIFFURED LADY: Yes, we were there the week. Well, it's very nearly the Arctic Circle. Oh yes, it was magnificent. The real deal!

HUSBAND: Red in tooth and claw!

COIFFURED LADY: Oh, I can't tell you! You know, these were *real* wolves, a *real* pack, and you're seeing them living out there in the wilds...

HUSBAND: Hunting, killing...

ANORAK LADY: Ooh, it sounds grand doesn't it, Michael?

MICHAEL: Aye.

COIFFURED LADY: Oh it was. And of course observing the wolves' behaviour teaches you *so* much about your own dog.

Telegraph Road

A couple are taking part in a discussion about music to drive to.

MIKE: I'm a sucker for old sixties stuff when I'm driving. You know, Motown, that kind of thing. Pulled up next to a lorry in a jam the other day and the driver starts singing along too.

LIZ: I like heavy stuff. I think I drive better when I've got something heavy on.

SHELLY: I'd stick with Radio Four but Cameron *has* to have music.

CAMERON: Best track ever for driving is 'Telegraph Road', Dire Straits. Fourteen minutes long. Lasts me exactly as long as the drive from Aston into work. Perfect.

SHELLY: Yeah, but you don't actually like the song though, do you, Cam?

CAMERON: No, but you're missing the point. It's fourteen minutes. That's exactly the same time it takes me to drive to work from home.

SHELLY: Yes, but you bloody hate it. You swear about it every day.

MIKE: Why not just get a couple of songs that you do like that add up to fourteen minutes and put them on a tape?

CAMERON: (exasperated) Look, you're not getting this, are you? It's fourteen minutes long!

Stranger in Town

A man ambles in to a post office clutching a bundle of papers. He joins the end of the long queue and catches the attention of the women in front of him.

MAN: Excuse me, do you know where the council offices are? It says in this letter that I've got to go to Pilgrim's Place.

OLD WOMAN: Pilgrim's Place? Pilgrim's Place! Oh yes, you go out of here to Market Square. Do you know where that is?

MAN: No, I don't know Bedford.

OLD WOMAN: Right. Do you know the Harper Centre?

MAN: No, I don't know Bedford.

OLD WOMAN: Do you know where Boots is?

MAN: No, I don't know Bedford.

OLD WOMAN: Hmmm.

SECOND WOMAN: There's no point us trying. He doesn't know Bedford!

'Spolicy

*A man is in an independent retailers stocking up with medicines.
He puts his purchases down in front of the checkout assistant.*

CHECKOUT: Oh, excuse me a minute, sir, I'll just need to call
the supervisor.

*The supervisor, who happens to be in earshot, strolls over and takes
a look at the four packs of paracetamol and one pack of aspirin.*

SUPERVISOR: That's okay, Mandy. Sir, I'm afraid we'll have
to process these as single purchases.

MAN: I have to pay for them separately?

SUPERVISOR: Yes, sir. 'Spolicy.

MAN: I don't understand. You mean you want me to do five
separate transactions with my debit card?

SUPERVISOR: Yes, sir. Sorry, sir, 'spolicy.

The people in the queue behind the man begins to mutter darkly.

MAN: But they're what? Forty pence each?

SUPERVISOR: Nothing I can do, sir. 'Scompany policy.

MAN: O-kay.

*The supervisor moves on. The queue mutters ever more darkly
behind the man as he falteringly proceeds with his purchases.*

MAN: So is this about preventing suicides or something?

CHECKOUT: Dunno. Just can't do it.

With all purchases made, the man offers a regretful smile to the grumpy elderly gentleman behind him in the queue.

ELDERLY GENTLEMAN: If the buggers want to die, bloody let 'em! That's what I say!

Muttered agreement along the length of the queue.

The Man Who Has Everything

Two girlfriends are at lunch.

1: I thought you were stuck on that accountant bloke.

2: No. Turns out he had a real fetish for Oriental women.

1: What about the pilot?

2: Jim? Rich Jim, the American? Oh, he wasn't a pilot, he just owned a few planes, a Ferrari, a vintage Morgan, a beach house in LA, a condo in Miami...

1: Hmm, the man who has everything, eh?

2: Exactly. Including a god-awful scar where his willy used to be. Bicycle accident when he was young.

1: Bicycle accident?

2: Yes. I mean you could forgive him a glorious motorbike accident, couldn't you? But not amputation by pushbike.

Snappy Shopper

Two middle-aged ladies are riding the lift in a bargain clothing store.

WOMAN 1: (tsk) Look at me! Thirty-two pounds just on underwear.

WOMAN 2: Oh give over! There's shops you can spend thirty-two pounds on a single bra!

WOMAN 1: (tutting) A single bra...I mean, it won't last and who's going to see it?

Woman 1 exits the lift, her friend following just behind.

WOMAN 2: You speak for yourself!

The Washing-line of Hope

An elderly mother and her thirty-something daughter are seating themselves at a street-side cafe.

MOTHER: Oh my word, you know I just can't cope with these shopping marathons any more. All these people!

DAUGHTER: Mmmm. I hate it when the sales are on. Everybody's just so rude. And the sale stuff is just rubbish! I didn't see a bloody thing I wanted all day.

MOTHER: Oh well, at least the one good thing that came out of today was that I managed to get that new washing line at last.

DAUGHTER: Well, that and Dad getting the all-clear from cancer.

MOTHER: Oh yes. There was that, wasn't there.

Scusting

Two teenagers are walking across the town centre dressed for a night out, hunched up against the cold and chatting loudly.

GIRL 1: I mean, I've seen Phil in the shower, I've seen Mick naked and I've seen Alan's bare arse. I'm telling you, I've seen it all!

GIRL 2: Ooh...

She shudders.

GIRL 1: And I'll tell you this an' all. It's scusting!

Memorable Elephants

An older couple recount a life-changing holiday.

MADELEINE: Oh my goodness... Delhi, Calcutta, the Taj Mahal - quite unforgettable.

JIM: And the elephants.

MADELEINE: Hmm?

JIM: The elephants.

MADELEINE: Oh, the elephants! Oh my goodness, yes, the elephants! I shall never, ever forget that experience. Oh yes, it makes me excited just to think about it. There we both were, on our elephants, just sort of gliding across the jungle.

JIM: Elephant.

MADELEINE: Hmmm?

JIM: Elephant. You said elephants.

MADELEINE: Yes well, there were two.

JIM: Yes, but we were riding on the same one.

MADELEINE: Hmm? Really? Oh yes, I suppose in a way we were. In a way. That's right, you were riding towards the back and I was on the shoulders. Leading the way, so to speak.

JIM: We were side by side. You were looking one way. I was facing the other. You nearly fell off.

MADELEINE: Well yes, I suppose so. In a way. But it was really quite delightful. A truly unforgettable experience.

The Endless Queue

Two elderly women wait in a long and slow checkout queue in a supermarket.

A: Oooh, I don't know. This is the worst bit of shopping, isn't it?

B: It is, love. Not that there's anybody waiting on me like.

A: Oh are you on your own too, love?

B: Aye, thirteen, nay, fourteen years now.

A: I'm a bit longer meself. You know, they say it gets better but it never does, does it?

B: No. You wait for it to get better but it doesn't. There's never nobody there when you get back, and when you're at home you never hear that sound of t'key in t'door any more. Miss him every day.

A: Aye.

B: Aye.

Two Birds Having It Off

A property PR person is talking to the MD of a building company and a female friend.

PR (to MD): You have to go away now. I need to spill some gossip to Jill.

MD: That's not fair, I never get to hear gossip. I don't get rude faxes, e-mails or anything. Go on, tell me.

PR: If you're sure.

MD: Absolutely.

PR: Well, the other day the sales negotiator here was outside having a lunchtime fag when she glanced across the bird sanctuary and realised that there were two women having full-on sex in the reeds.

MD: Christ!

PR: Anyway, the sales negotiator is so shocked by this that she just has to tell someone. So she runs into the office and phones the site manager and tells him there are two birds having it off in the sanctuary. He says, 'So what?', then he realises she means two women, not two chaffinches. *Now* he's interested. Anyway, in his rush to get down there and have a good old look he takes a corner too tightly and writes off his car—

MD: A brand-new Land Rover.

PR: That's right!

MD: That would be a company car then?

PR: (sigh) You see! That's why you never get to hear gossip!

Multicultural, innit?

A son is guiding his northern father around on his first trip to London.

FATHER: Tha' know, son, I don't think I've ever seen so many Pakis in one place before.

SON: Dad! You can't go around calling people Pakis.

FATHER: Well, what am I supposed to call 'em then?

SON: You don't have to call them anything! This is London, there's loads of people from all over, and you wouldn't know most of them were foreign till they opened their mouths.

FATHER: That may be so, but you can spot Pakis, can't you?

SON: Dad!

FATHER: I were just making an observation! It's right multicultural, innit?

SON: The least you can do is say there's lots of people from Pakistan or something.

FATHER: All right. All right.

A few minutes later, they're in a queue for tickets at the tube station when the father nudges his son.

FATHER: There you go, son. I think that *person from Pakistan* is ready to serve you now.

The Hot Date

In a supermarket checkout queue an elderly lady points to her purchase – an organically reared chicken.

ELDERLY LADY: Oh they're lovely they are! Really succulent. Just enough for me and a red setter!

S&M in the High Street

A sales counter in a department store. An older shop assistant with a Yorkshire accent serves a young woman.

ASSISTANT: 'ello, love! You shopping?

YOUNG WOMAN: Yeah. Got a party to go to. Thought I'd treat myself to a new outfit.

The assistant looks a little shocked and lifts up the young woman's purchases.

ASSISTANT: Knickers and um 'andbag? By 'eck, love. I hope you're wearing more than that!

Romance

A miffed office worker puts the phone down.

SARAH: Oooh! Northern men!

RACHEL: S'up, love, 'as he upset you?

SARAH: Oooh, no more than usual! I 'aven't seen him for three weeks and I 'aven't spoken to him for two, and I'm telling him how much I miss him and that I love him and do you know what he says?

RACHEL: Go on.

SARAH: He says 'similar'. Five bloody years we've been together and he says 'similar'. Men!

Rice

Dad is just serving up a not-terribly appealing lunch.

DAD: There you go! Amazing all this, isn't it? I mean, imagine being able to freeze rice. Fantastic.

TOMMY: (poking the contents of his plate nervously) Dad, how did you cook this?

DAD: What, the rice? You just bung it in a pan of boiling water for fifteen minutes or so.

TOMMY: But Dad, doesn't ordinary rice take 15 minutes to cook?

DAD: Oh I don't know. Perhaps.

TOMMY: But, Dad, if you boil frozen rice for fifteen minutes doesn't it turn into a gluey, sticky mass like this?

DAD: (peeved) Well I thought it was all right!

TOMMY: Dad, if you're cooking the ordinary rice and frozen rice for the same amount of time, then what is the point of having frozen rice?

DAD: Well you can store it in the freezer, can't you!

Taking Stock

A group of old friends are taking stock at a wedding.

RYAN: I mean, this is beautiful and everything. It feels like these two, you know... You know what I mean? But look at us. Jesus. This finishes at twelve and where are we going then? Bed! BED! What happens? I mean, what happened to the kids who couldn't get enough of everything? You know, EVERYTHING! Drugs, booze, the lot. What happens? How does it happen?

CRAIG: I don't know, mate, it just does. Anybody want a last one?

CARL: I could squeeze half in.

TESS: Orange juice, please!

RYAN: Yeah, go on then. Mineral water for me, thanks.

Public Inconvenience

A nuclear family is browsing through the bathroom displays at their local DIY store.

DAD: That'd look good.

MUM: Dunno. Might be a bit, you know.

DAD: Suppose so.

DAUGHTER: Mummy, I used the loo!

MUM: (to Dad). What do you think of that tub? Not the taps just the tub.

DAD: I don't like the taps.

MUM: Not the taps, just the tub.

DAD: It's just a tub, isn't it?

DAUGHTER: Mummy, Mummy! I used the loo.

MUM: Shhhhh! Yes, darling, I heard you the first time. Look, I'll take you in a minute. Mummy and Daddy want to look at the bathtubs.

Their baby son in his pushchair begins to whine.

DAD: Oh now look!

DAUGHTER: Mummy, I did it in the loo.

MUM: Isabelle, stop shouting! Look, you've woken your brother now! All Daddy and me wanted to do was to have five minutes looking at bathtubs, but oh no! Come on then, madam, let's find you a loo.

DAUGHTER: Mummy, I used the loo!

DAD: What is she talking about?

MUM: I don't know, she says she used the– Oh. Isabelle, darling, which loo did you use?

DAUGHTER: (pointing to a display) That one!

MUM: Oh you didn't. Tell me you didn't.

She opens the loo lid.

MUM: Oh for god's sake, Isabelle!

Controversy

A former high-profile female politician at lunch.

POLITICIAN: It breaks my heart. You wouldn't believe how many MPs are gay, the married ones too. It breaks my heart. Good, normal men made to hide their true feelings like this because the blue rinse and rubber chicken brigade out in the constituencies think it's against nature. It's barbaric. So much of Parliament, the Lords especially, is like that though. It's the 1990s and yet they still spend hours and hours debating whether or not the Lord Chancellor should have to wear tights. Is it any wonder that I got fed up?

Potty

*An expensively coiffured lady of a certain age and an
elderly gentleman are waiting outside the garden centre shop.*

LADY: Where's Izzy got to?

GENTLEMAN: I think she's just popped back into the shop.
Pots, I think.

LADY: Oh, really.

GENTLEMAN: Well you can never have enough pots, can you?

LADY: Oh my goodness, yes! I *hate* pots! I *hate* them! Ghastly
things cluttering up the garden! I *hate* them!

GENTLEMAN: Oh well, I'm sure she won't be long...

LADY: I mean, why on earth do people persist with the ghastly
things? *I HATE POTS!*

GENTLEMAN: Right, well, I'm sure she won't be long.

The lady shudders.

LADY: And don't get me started on containers!

Parenthood

Parents discuss their parenting experiences over a cuppa in the staff room.

LAURA: I'm having such a battle with Ella at the moment. Every morning I have to ask her three or four times to do something. This morning she ran off and hid behind the door so I couldn't brush her hair.

The others laugh.

LAURA: I know it *is* funny but you can't show amusement in situations like that, can you?

JEN: With us it's bedtimes and brushing teeth.

DEPARTMENT HEAD: I find mornings and evenings a nightmare. And the weekends. The bits when they're asleep are pretty okay.

JEN: What are you saying? Those perfect little boys!

DEPARTMENT HEAD: Perfect? Have you met my two? Michael is all surly and 'You don't look after meeeee!' And Aidan would just lob an axe at you if he had one.

JEN: Well I have to say Ben spent rather a lot of yesterday evening on the naughty step.

The department technician, mother of adult sons snorts.

DEPARTMENT TECHNICIAN: Wish I could still put my Jacob on the naughty step!

Over-inflated

A man is being assisted in the purchase of several helium-filled balloons by a shop assistant, Clare, who is young, tall and wiry. As she fills the last balloon she calls over to her workmate Maddie.

CLARE: Come on, Maddie, you've got to learn how to do this sometime so it might as well be now.

MADDIE: Oooh.

Maddie, who is short and curvaceous, squeezes into the ridiculously tiny area behind the counter where the helium tank is mounted. Standing together they look like the figure '18'.

CLARE: Don't worry, you can't go wrong.

MADDIE: Oooh, I don't know.

CLARE: You know, *I* had to do it on me very first day!

MADDIE: I don't want to burst it.

CLARE: You won't! Look, you put this bit on here, right?

MADDIE: Like that?

CLARE: Bit further... That's it, go on then.

Pssstttttt.

CLARE: That's it, go on! You can't over-inflate it!

Pstttttttt.
52

MADDIE: How will I know when it's done?

CLARE: Oh you'll know, don't worry! Now, just step back a bit so it can fill up.

Maddie steps back as far as she can, but there is still not enough room for the balloon to inflate between the helium cylinder and her tummy.

MADDIE: Oh right, er, maybe if you...

Maddie sucks in her tummy and crushes her buttocks against the wall, only for her enormous breasts to fill the available space.

Clare bites her lip.

CLARE: You know, maybe we'll have another go at this a bit later.

Not the Done Thing

A casual agency worker working a double shift yawns, stretches and goes back to work at the mail-sorting office just as the day shift are arriving.

MALE SORTING OFFICE WORKER: 'Ere, mate, what you doin'?

AGENCY WORKER: Er, sorting?

MALE SORTING OFFICE WORKER: (laughing) Not like that, you're not!

FEMALE SORTING OFFICE WORKER: Leave him alone, Frank. 'e's casual, 'e's not to know.

AGENCY WORKER: I'm sorry, am I doing something wrong?

MALE SORTING OFFICE WORKER: Aye!

FEMALE SORTING OFFICE WORKER: You're on the wrong side, love. You stand this side of the table.

AGENCY WORKER: Erm, look, I've worked three night shifts in a row and nobody else has told me I'm on the wrong side of the table.

MALE SORTING OFFICE WORKER: What's 'e say?

FEMALE SORTING OFFICE WORKER: 'e says no one else has told 'im 'e's at the wrong side.

MALE SORTING OFFICE WORKER: Daft.

FEMALE SORTING OFFICE WORKER: But you can't have worked that side, love, you'd be in everybody else's way.

AGENCY WORKER: No, it was fine. We were all on this side.

FEMALE SORTING OFFICE WORKER: You what?

MALE SORTING OFFICE WORKER: What's 'e say?

FEMALE SORTING OFFICE WORKER: 'E says they were all on that side. What, love? Gaffer too? Every day?

AGENCY WORKER: Yeah. Why?

FEMALE SORTING OFFICE WORKER: Well I'm blowed! Did you 'ear that, Frank? He says night shift works on that side of the table!

MALE SORTING OFFICE WORKER: He didn't!

FEMALE SORTING OFFICE WORKER: He did! Tell 'im, love! Tell 'im what you just told me!

AGENCY WORKER: The night shift works on this side of the table.

MALE SORTING OFFICE WORKER: Well I'll go t'foot of our stairs. I never knew that! I've been here twenty-odd years and I never knew that.

FEMALE SORTING OFFICE WORKER: You know, I'm shocked! Why didn't nobody ever tell us?

MALE SORTING OFFICE WORKER: I tell you, I'm gobsmacked.

FEMALE SORTING OFFICE WORKER: You know, I think I need a sit down!

Nah, Mate!

A man is making a phone call on a train halted at Farringdon station.

MAN: Mick?

Steve.

Done.

All done.

Nah, mate.

Seven-fifty.

Nah, mate, I said seven-fifty.

Nah, mate.

Nah, mate.

Nah, mate.

Look, I 'ad to buy the pick-up for a start, that was three hundred.

Three hundred.

Three.

Nah, mate, couldn't do it.

We said seven-fifty. Naaaaaaah.

What then?

Two fifty?

Two fifty?! Naaaaaaaaah, mate, we said seven fifty!

Seven.

Seven then.

Nah, mate, couldn't do it.

Six-fifty.

Nah, mate.

Nah, mate.

Nah, mate.

Nah, mate. Two-fifty? You're 'aving a larf!

Two-fifty?

Two bloody fifty?

(Silence)

Yeah, go on then, two-fifty.

Cheers.

Sweet!

He disconnects.

Mothers

Competitive mothers of four year olds go head-to-head.

MOTHER A: Unusual for Tati but she didn't like ice-skating. She said that it was cold, nasty and wet and she wasn't going again.

MOTHER B: Pippa just *adored* it, she wouldn't let me hold her hand and she was amazing. But I suppose it helps that she skis.

MOTHER A: Hmm. At least it gave Tatianna something to write about in her diary. Did I mention she was keeping a diary?

MOTHER B: How sweet! Of course Pippa has been keeping a journal.

MOTHER A: Oh...fancy.

MOTHER C: (under her breath in sing-song voice to her child) Those mothers should be shot shouldn't they, sweetums?

The Celebrity and the Portaloo

Two stylists have been comparing notes on people that they've worked with.

STYLIST 1: You know she likes to film in her own kitchen? Well she's got this kind of conservatory kitchen and said that we could use that. Well, everything was fine, but then she said that she was fed up with the crew using her loo and tramping mud over everything, and that we'd have to bring in a portaloo for the crew to use. So they did. Thing is, as they're lifting this portaloo into place with a crane, her cat gets underneath and SPLAT.

STYLIST 2: No!

STYLIST 1: Yup. I mean, I felt awful for her and obviously the cat... But honestly, it was such a stupid accident that half the crew were trying not to crack up.

Tourist Information

A busy street outside a London mainline station.

NEWS VENDOR: Get 'em while they're hot, tomorrow's news today. Yes, sir? What can I do you for?

TOURIST: 'Scuz' pliz. The Buckingham's Palace?

NEWS VENDOR: Gordon Benn— Do I look like a facking policeman? Well do I? Fack, off and buy yourself an A–Z like a normal human being!

TOURIST: Pliz?

NEWS VENDOR: (pointing) One of them, you dozy, dago Kraut.

TOURIST: (picking up a London A–Z) Yes?

NEWS VENDOR: Jesus, mother and— What does it say on the bleeding cover? Are you mental as well as ugly?

TOURIST: Ah, senk you!

Tourist turns up his MP3 player and makes off slowly with the A–Z. Incensed, the news vendor gives chase.

NEWS VENDOR: 'Ere! Come back 'ere you dozy French cant!

The news vendor collides with one of his own magazine racks, knocking it over.

NEWS VENDOR: Cor! Try and be decent to people and look what facking happens, eh?

A passing old lady appears upset by a gay porn magazine that has fallen open on the floor. The news vendor snatches it up.

NEWS VENDOR: Don't tell me you ain't see one them before! Not at your age! Go on! Get out of it!

Jimmy Scumbag's Report

A drunk and disgruntled new teacher is heading home on a train passing through Bexleyheath.

TEACHER: Well I'm leaving, so what do I care? You know, I did forty reports last night, and half of the names I couldn't even put a face to. They did all right out of it actually – I just cut and pasted the same remarks for them all, then jigged them around a bit for variety. I left a legacy behind too though. All those little bleeders who messed me around for the last three terms, I added stuff like 'continually picks his nose' or 'prefers exposing herself to her classmates to wrestling with literature'. Thing is, these reports are legal documents, so they can't be altered afterwards. Which means anyone whose interested, for ever more, can look up little Jimmy Scumbag's report and see that he was considered antisocially flatulent at school.

Man's Best Friend

India, an art dealer, is taking Hannah, a wealthy, elderly client, to view work by a new artist at a joint exhibition. On the way they pass a series of large black and white photographs – close-ups of the artist's penis.

HANNAH: Oh look, isn't that darling!

INDIA: Er. Mmmm.

HANNAH: Oh look at its little nose! What breed do you suppose it is?

INDIA: Oh, er, well it's difficult to tell...

HANNAH: Oh I do love them at that age! So much potential ahead of them. You know, I thought I was too old, but now I'm really thinking I should get another one.

INDIA: Hannah? You do know what that is, don't you?

HANNAH: Well I was thinking it was a Labrador but now I'm thinking it might be one of those wrinkly Oriental ones. Lord, what are they called?

Hannah bends to look at the description next to the photograph.

HANNAH: (quickly walking away) Well. I think that's quite enough time spent here.

Tea? Coffee?

A young family are visiting grandma.

GRANDMA: Oooh, it is lovely to see you all. Eh, I bet you're gasping for a drink, aren't you?

SON: Actually I'm okay, Mum.

DAUGHTER-IN-LAW: Me too. They have like a buffet service on trains these days Sarah. We had a posh coffee just before we got off.

GRANDMA: Well what about the kids?

DAUGHTER-IN-LAW: They're fine. They've got juice and water. Now, come and sit down and say hello properly.

GRANDMA: (wringing her hands through a tea towel) Oh but you must be needing something. There's tea, coffee...
I got some of that coffee you said you like!

SON: What? Lavazza?

GRANDMA: That's it! Nescafé! You said you liked that!

SON: That's very sweet, Mum, but we're fine honest.

GRANDMA: Oh and I bought it special too...I've got juice! You know, squash like. Orange, lemon and lime, and blackcurrant cordial.

SON: Honestly, Mum, maybe later.

GRANDMA: Or there's pop! Cream soda, lemonade, orangeade, cola, and what's that other one...? (wanders off to kitchen)

DAUGHTER-IN-LAW: Sarah, come and sit down, love, we're fine, honestly.

GRANDMA: (returning triumphantly) Dandelion and burdock! Would you like a dandelion and burdock?

SON: We're trying to keep off the sugary stuff, Mum.

GRANDMA: (scrutinising the label) Sugar? Where does it say there's sugar in it? It's got saccharin, I think. You won't put on any weight with saccharin, love... Or there's milk? Chocolate? Horlicks? Cocoa? I mean, I know they're nighttime drinks but it can't do any harm, can it?

DAUGHTER-IN-LAW: Actually, Sarah, if there's a glass of white wine I wouldn't say no.

GRANDMA: Well I've got that Asti stuff from last Christmas. Bit too much for one...

DAUGHTER-IN-LAW: No you're right, Sarah. Tell you what, I'd love a big glass of water if that's okay?

GRANDMA: Tap water?

DAUGHTER-IN-LAW: Whatever you've got will be fine.

GRANDMA: You can't travel all this way and have tap water, love! Let me put a bit of squash in it for you.

DAUGHTER-IN-LAW: Lovely.

GRANDMA: (to son) And what about you?

SON: Okay, you've talked me into it. I'll have a lemonade please.

GRANDMA: (delighted) You see, I knew you must be gagging! Why didn't you just ask, you daft buggers? Now... What would you like to eat?

Innocence

A group of mums have been discussing their attempts to retain some youthful innocence in their children in the face of consumerism.

SALLY: But you can't win. For Christmas my Mum bought Alice some knickers from the Disney Store. You know, Santa prezzie, not the big prezzie. Anyway, they've got that cat from… whatsit called?

JO: Oh, you mean the one from *Aristocats*? Ginny's got those too!

SALLY: That's it! Anyway, Alice wakes up Christmas morning and she's absolutely delighted with these new knickers and she takes off her pyjamas, puts a pair on and starts dancing around the house in them.

JO: Aw, sweet!

SALLY: Well she's doing this thing she calls a sexy dance she's picked up off one of her friends.

JO: Eugh!

SALLY: Yes well, quite! Anyway, then Grandma turns up and Alice shimmies into the living room, starts grinding her pelvis, points at her crotch and shouts at the top of her voice, 'Hey, Grandma, look at my pussy!'

The other mums in the room clap hands over mouths.

SALLY: *I know!* And the thing is, she meant it completely innocently! Of couse! But lord, you should have seen the look I got off Grandma!

Maltesers

Two students are chatting about their grandparents on a bus to Milton Keynes.

STUDENT 1: My gran was nuts. She wouldn't ask for any kind of help, ever. She was so fiercely independent that it actually became a real bind, if you know what I mean. You never knew what trouble she was going to get into next. One weekend she's trying to change her curtains and she falls down and breaks her arm. Doesn't tell anyone for three days. My dad turns up to visit and she's there with her arm in a hand-made sling, it was broken in two places. She said, 'Oh, I didn't want to be a burden.' Nuts.

STUDENT 2: My gran was nuts too. She had this thing that when she went shopping she'd buy exactly the same stuff every week, biscuits and stuff, and then just put it in the left-hand side of the sideboard. When stuff she was using ran out she'd just reach down and take the first packet from the right-hand side. She never looked in the sideboard to see what she had or how long it had been in there, just kept filling it up. Course then it starts sliding around and getting mixed up. In the end some of it had been in there for years. I swear I was twelve before I realised that Maltesers were supposed to be crunchy.

History Repeating Itself

When the husband of their heavily pregnant and overdue friend takes his daughter to school, Rachel and Jill fix him with intense questioning stares. Eventually he notices.

HUSBAND: Oh no, no, no! No, nothing yet, she's just having a lie-in.

JILL: When we saw you we thought, 'ello she's started.

HUSBAND: No, no, no. Mind you, Braxtons were going on for so long last night that we almost called the midwife...

RACHEL: Then it stopped.

HUSBAND: Then it stopped.

RACHEL: Well, that's it then, it's definitely a boy.

JILL: Yeah.

RACHEL: Boys always keep you waiting. Then they're toddlers and they keep you waiting. Then they grow up a bit and they keep you waiting. And then they're men... And then they keep you waiting! Oh yeah, it's gonna be a boy all right.

Two days later, the baby is born safe and well. It was a girl.

Mad as a Bee

An irritated young man is overheard talking to a friend on a slow commuter train.

MAN: My mum phoned me last night.

FRIEND: Oh yeah? How is she?

MAN: Mad as a bee since Dad died.

FRIEND: Yeah?

MAN: Yeah. Called me last night and she says, 'What's my next-door neighbours called?' 'Marion and Ray' I say, 'Why?' She says, 'No, I know that! What's their surname?' I say, 'I don't know, I just know them as Marion and Ray.' She says, 'Well your dad's written Hayes in the book.' 'Well it's probably Hayes then.' I say. 'But I thought it was Haye, H.a.y.e,' she says. 'There's not much in it.' I say. 'Why do you want to know?' 'Well your sister wants to send them a thank-you card for the baby clothes they sent her, but we don't know who to address it to,' she says. 'Well address it to Marion and Ray at their house next door.' I say. 'You know the address!' 'Ooh, I don't know,' she says. 'Do you think they'll get it if I don't put the surname on?' 'It's a bloody semi-detached house, Mum, they're the only people living there, of course they'll bloody get it,' I tell her. 'Oh well,' she says, 'as long as you're sure.' Mad!

Goths

The gothically disposed Alana raises her hand during an art lesson.

ALANA: Miss. Is Van Gogh spelt G.O.T.H as in goth?

MRS GREEN: No, Alana. It's spelt G.O.G.H not like goth as in Gothic.

ALANA: (sniffy) And what's wrong with goths?

MRS GREEN: Absolutely nothing. In fact, my husband used to be one.

TIM: Your husband? What, Mr Watts?

MRS GREEN: Nooo, Tim. *Mr Watts* is married to *Mrs Watts*. Mr Watts is simply my department head. We *work* together. We are *not* married. Contrary to popular opinion, not *all* teachers are married to each other.

TIM: Do you mean Mrs Watts the Italian teacher?

MRS GREEN: (sighing) I think we'd better stop this conversation now.

Arsebergers

A dad is in a play park with his autistic spectrum son. The park is deserted but a man in bike leathers is rolling a cigarette at a picnic table, while his young son, Jamie, chases a cat. Before the dad can stop him, his son picks up a large pile of wood chippings from beneath the swings and hurls it into the air, some landing very close to the man.

DAD: I'm sorry! He's autistic and this is his thing at the minute. I'll move him further away.

MAN: 'S'all right, mate. Didn't do no damage. Say 'es aut'istic?

Points to his own son, Jamie.

MAN: Arsebergers.

DAD: Ah, right. Small world!

MAN: I mean I'm a fackin' railway worker. Wot the fackin' 'ell do I know? Doin' the missus' 'ed in. Well, I mean she's not my missus. I mean we're not married nor nothing.

DAD: Uh-uh.

MAN: Fing is, I can't see it lasting neither. Jus' don't like each other *really*... An' this?

Indicates Jamie.

MAN: Love 'im an' 'all but fackin' 'ell! 'E don't go to the loo.

Y'know, number twos. Days e goes. Nathin'. Fackin' miserable 'e is. Fackin' uncomfortable. Well, you would be, wouldn' you?

Jamie finally gets a good hold of the cat's tail.

MAN: JAMIE! LEAV' 'IM ALONE 'E DUN LIKE IT! LEAVE! 'IM! ALONE! Poor fackin' thing. 'E don't know when to leave 'em alone.

DAD: Not easy, is it?

The man rolls his eyes.

MAN: We went to fackin' Cyprus last year. 'Er family. Ain't bin on 'oliday since... (makes hand gesture). Fackin' needed it, mate! Anyway, he ain't bin to the loo about four days or sumfink. Where we is they ain't got fackin' flash loos like we 'ave. Fackin 'ole, innit? Anyway, he fackin' decides it's time, and I'm telling ya mate, when this fackin' thing drops out it's like a fackin' football. 'E's screamin'! 'Ad ta fackin force it down the 'ole with a fackin stick. course it fackin' blocks the fackin' sewer, don't it? Whole fackin' village. Oh, we're poplar!

The man goes quiet, lights his cigarette. He appears to get smoke in his eyes.

It's the Thought That Counts

Flatmates are discussing their worst-ever Christmas gifts.

MATT: Mine was well intentioned, but you know how parents just always get it wrong?

CHRIS: Oh yes!

MATT: Well, I was only about ten, and I'd just inherited my brother's old cassette player – a real antique, even then, but I was chuffed with it. Anyway, for Christmas I asked for some TDK tapes to do some recording. *Hawaii Five-O* music off the telly and stuff. Thing is, mum being mum, she thinks that instead of getting a pack of three tapes for like, three pounds or whatever they were, it would be a much better idea to go to a cheapy cheap shop and buy me thirty tapes for the exact same money. Not one of the bastards worked. And I had to spend all Boxing Day trying to free mangled tape from the cassette player.

CHRIS: I once made the cardinal error of saying I was interested in guitars to my auntie. I mean, I play guitar, but I wouldn't say I was interested in them per se. Anyway, every year for the last five years she's been sending me this book, *Guitar Serial Numbers*, which is a book full of guitar serial numbers.

MATT: That's bad, but I think your brick of soap last year was the worst ever.

CHRIS: That was bad, wasn't it? Useful bad, though. I mean, I do use it, so it's not like fridge magnet bad, is it?

DAN: Oh, mate, that soap is ridiculous. It's fucking huge! When I'm in the shower I sometimes look down and think, 'Fuck, I'm soaping my bollocks with a fucking great brick of soap.' Mate, you're going to have to cut it into bits or something.

CHRIS: (trying not to be sick) Yeah, that's not a bad idea.

DAN: (getting up) Anybody want another beer?

MATT: Please!

CHRIS: Oh yes.

Dan leaves the room.

MATT: You've got to throw that soap away.

CHRIS: Oh, yes!

Learning by Example

A young father admonishes his young son on a busy high street.

FATHER: How many fucking times do I have to tell you? Don't fucking swear!

Fast Food

A young man in front of the counter at a burger restaurant takes a call on his mobile.

YOUNG MAN: 'Allo, sweets. Yeah, I'm coming over. Macdonal's. Want me to get you anyfink? Milkshake?' So don't 'ave one! 'M not... 'M not! Soyawananyfink? Yeah butdoyawananyfink? No? So nothink? Fries. All right fries... Dunno, chicken legend thing... Well, wot? No... Soyawananyfink?

He turns round briefly to the man behind him in the queue.

YOUNG MAN: Soz mate. So... Soyawananyfink? Yeah, butdoyawananyfink? Chicken legend, yeah? Fries, yeah?

He turns to the heavily accented fast food worker who has been waiting patiently to take his order.

YOUNG MAN: Yeah, mate, caniave chicken legend?

FAST FOOD WORKER: Mayonnaise?

YOUNG MAN: Yeah, fries.

FAST FOOD WORKER: You want fries with that?

YOUNG MAN: What?

He indicates his phone.

YOUNG MAN: Sodoyawananyfink? Milkshake. Flavour?

(To fast food worker) Cheers, mate, chocolate milkshake, yeah? Nah, mate, *vanilla*! (to phone). Look, gottago. Yeah, gottago. Right, see ya, sweets. Yeah?

He disconnects, shakes his head.

YOUNG MAN: Fack!

FAST FOOD WORKER: I'm sorry, sir, so you're wanting a chocolate milkshake, two vanilla milkshakes, a chicken legend with mayonnaise and fries..?

YOUNG MAN: Nah, nah, nah...

The young man stands open-mouthed, and scratches his head, brain-fried.

YOUNG MAN: Oh *fack*!

It Takes Me Back

A group of mums at a toddler group juggle kids and coffee.

KAREN: God, honestly, kids are such a liability! I've just had an argument with Amanda at the bus stop. She said to me, 'Mummy, look at that big fat woman.' And I have to admit the woman next to us was huge. And I said, 'No she's not' trying not to die of embarrassment. And then Amanda gets angry, screaming at the top of her lungs, 'Yes she is, Mummy! She's fat!'

CHRISTY: I know, I wonder what goes through their little minds? The other day I was in a bookshop and Jacob picks up this book, holds it up and says, 'Oooh that takes me back.' Back to when?! Last summer? He's three, for heaven's sake!

Esmerelda

Two elderly ladies are on a train to Norwich. At an intermediary station one lady notices a row of luggage trolleys, each of which has a name scrawled across it in felt tip pen. The lady points to one clearly called 'Esmerelda'.

FIRST LADY: Ooh, look, Elsie! That trolley's called Imelda.

ELSIE: Ooh, fancy! You know Ruth was really an Imelda, don't you?

FIRST LADY: Is that Ruth who went to Canada?

ELSIE: Basingstoke, yes. She had a dodgy terrier. Walked with a stick.

FIRST LADY: Would she fetch the stick?

ELSIE: Oh aye! She was a *he*, mind.

FIRST LADY: (shocked) Fancy!

ELSIE: She never did find that brooch of hers, you know?

FIRST LADY: No?

ELSIE: No.

FIRST LADY: Oh.

Good Genes ain't Everything

A very good-looking, taller, blonder and fitter than average couple are being talked through home ovulation kits by an assistant at a high street chemist.

ASSISTANT: Well, as you can see, there's a wide range of products that can predict ovulation, but they all pretty much work on the same principle. This one, for example, has these little sticks that you wee on and they turn colour when you're ovulating.

MAN: Do we both have to wee on the same one, or one each?

Uncomfortable silence.

ASSISTANT: Well of course, full instructions are included.

A Building Term

Saturday morning at the supermarket. Sophie, a very charming little girl of around seven, is merrily pirouetting in front of the cashier while her mum loads groceries from her trolley onto the conveyor belt. The little girl has a small brown wage packet in her hands, which, as the time comes to pay, she offers to the cashier.

SOPHIE: It's okay, Mummy, I'll pay.

CASHIER: Oh, that's very grown-up of you! I wish my little girl would offer to pay for the shopping now and then.

MUM: That's very sweet of you, darling, but I'm not sure you're going to have quite enough. (To cashier) We've got the builders in and Sophie's been helping them move things and offering a bit of advice now and then.

CASHIER: Oh that must be nice for them!

MUM: Yeeeees. Anyway, yesterday all the site men got paid and the foreman gave her her own wage packet with a couple of quid in it for being so helpful. So sweet of him.

CASHIER: (to Sophie) Oh what a clever girl! Well, you must have been very helpful indeed for him to pay you like the other chaps.

Sophie nods and giggles charmingly. By now, several aisles in the supermarket are fully engaged with the tale.

CASHIER: And are you going to help them next week as well?

SOPHIE: (very serious) Yes. But the foreman says we can't do a thing until those fucking bricks are delivered.

Silence, punctuated only by the beep of groceries being scanned.

Giving Direction

A householder listens to a message on his answer machine.

Beep.

MAN: You cut me off, man! Look, when you get to Victoria you get the tube, yeah? Victoria line up to St Pancras, yeah? Then you got to change, man. Get on the Northern Line southbound to Angel, yeah? Then you cross the road over to where the Body Shop is, yeah and there's a bus stop and you want the 141 or the 73. If you get the 141 you gotta get off at the park, yeah? Soon as you see the park you get off, and you cross the road and you walk down Stoke Newington High Street, okay? That's where we is... If you get the 73 you gotta ask the conductor to let you off the stop before Stoke Newington High Street, yeah? Then you walk down Stoke Newington High Street and there we is, yeah? Two o'clock. You got me, yeah? Man, you better turn up this time or you better just forget it, like for ever, yeah? I ain't waiting for you no more. And bring the stuff, yeah? All right. Later.

It's a wrong number.

Battery-powered

A mother and father are talking to a single friend outside a cafe in Kensington.

FATHER: Kids are a constant source of bemusement.
Take last month, one of the twins had what we thought was a throat infection, so we whisked him off to the doctors, fed him the antibiotics and everything, but nothing happened.

MOTHER: It was really beginning to get him down, poor little mite, and we weren't getting much sleep so we took him to see a specialist. Anyway, the specialist has a root around his throat and then his nose. Then he gets out a long pair of tweezers and, sticking them up his nostril, plucks out this zinc watch battery that the other twin has stuck up there for safe-keeping.

FRIEND: Oh my word!

MOTHER: Well exactly! Anyway, we take them home and give them both a stern lecture about not doing anything so silly again, then forget about it.

FATHER: Only, Luke isn't getting any better. He's still got a sore throat, he's only really able to breathe properly through his mouth, and he's still keeping us up all night. So we go back to the doctors and get more antibiotics, assuming that it's an infection from having the battery up there. But after another couple of days he seems to be getting worse, not better.

MOTHER: Anyway, so now we're getting a bit frantic, so we go back to see the specialist as quick as we can. Literally, we're just rolling off the driveway when Luke pipes up, 'Daddy? This time, can you ask him to take the other battery out too?'

Generation XXX

A young boy in skater gear and heavily gelled hair is walking through the park with his immaculately turned out and bored-looking grandparents.

BOY: Yeah, yeah, and then he stuck a knife in me, in me eye, and then right, right, he opened up me 'ead and started scooping out me brains with a spoon, right?

GRANDFATHER: (sighing) Yes, well, that wouldn't have taken him very long, would it?

Balham?

A ticket examiner has stopped a young man who does not have a ticket at Victoria Station ticket barrier.

TICKET EXAMINER: Now, sir, you don't have a ticket, which makes you liable for an on-the-spot £10 fine...

YOUNG MAN: Oh, man!

TICKET EXAMINER: However, as today is my birthday and I am in a good mood, I am going to allow you to purchase a ticket from me for your journey at the usual price instead. That okay?

YOUNG MAN: That's decent of you, man, cheers!

TICKET EXAMINER: Not at all, sir. Now, can you tell me which station you got on at please, sir?

YOUNG MAN: Er, yeah, it was um Battersea Park.

TICKET EXAMINER regards the young man silently for an uncomfortably long period of time.

YOUNG MAN: Oh! No! What am I thinking, no, of course it wasn't. I got *on* at Wandsworth. Sorry, I'm still half-asleep.

TICKET EXAMINER: Only half, sir? So Wandsworth, eh?

YOUNG MAN: That's right.

TICKET EXAMINER: I don't think it was, you know, sir.

YOUNG MAN: Sorry, you're right. I mean Clapham Junction. I've just moved, man, I get them mixed up.

TICKET EXAMINER: Big difference between Clapham Junction and Wandsworth I'd say, sir. Big difference. Why don't you give it another go?

YOUNG MAN: Er. Balham?

TICKET EXAMINER: (winces)

YOUNG MAN: Streatham?

TICKET EXAMINER: Tsk tsk tsk.

YOUNG MAN: Streatham Hill?

TICKET EXAMINER: (sighing) Help me out a little bit, sir.

Gazebo

A young family and their Mother emerge from a coffee and muffin shop and wander into a catalogue shopping outlet where a garden furniture display dominates the floor.

SON: 'Ere, Mum, fancy a gazebo?

MUM: (patting her stomach) Ooh no, love, I couldn't.

Dullest Cat Food Story in the World

An elderly and rather rotund mother and her equally rotund daughter are ambling back towards the supermarket car park with their shopping.

MOTHER: You know Sooty doesn't like the tinned stuff. Turns his nose up he does. Even at the expensive ones.

DAUGHTER: No!

MOTHER: He does! Wouldn't touch it at all. He had a lick of it the first couple of times but now he won't touch it. I tried some of that stuff in pouches. That's expensive!

DAUGHTER: And did he like that?

MOTHER: No! Waste of money! But I did try the dried food and he does like that. Particularly the rabbit. I swear, I've never known a cat like it.

DAUGHTER: Oooh, but they are fussy creatures, aren't they?

MOTHER: Aren't they?

DAUGHTER: They are.

MOTHER: I *know* they are!

DAUGHTER: Yeah.

MOTHER: Yeah.

Front or Back Bottom?

On a crowded train between London and Birmingham, a power-dressed Mother makes a phone call home in a very loud voice.

MOTHER: Darling? It's Mummy, darling. How are you? Good. Now, have you had a poo? You're not sure? Well, does Daddy think you've had a poo? Daddy was watering the azaleas, was he? Well, did nanny see? Nanny's not there yet, I see. Well, what about Thomas? Darling, please concentrate, did Thomas look and see if you'd had a poo or not? He didn't. But you did go to the toilet like I asked you to? Yes? Good girl. And when you were on the toilet what did you do? You sang? That's lovely, darling, but what did you do in the toilet? Front or back bottom? Darling, it's called a front bottom because it's at the front. Now, which one did you go to the toilet out of? You're not sure. Well, did you have a look afterward? And what colour was it? Well then, that's not really a poo is it, darling? Sugarplum, will you do Mummy a big favour and go and sit on the toilet again, right now? Yes, I know you've got to go to school, but we don't want another accident now, do we? Are you there? No, you have to pull them all the way down, darling, halfway won't do. Right, are you sitting? Good. Yes, you can sing if you want to, darling. Now, I want you to tell me *everything* that's happening...

Death of a Hamster

At the school gates, children run around, the mums chat

DEBRA: Hi, Steph. Good weekend?

STEPH: Well, it was a bit traumatic

DEBRA: Why, what happened? It was Kieran's birthday, wasn't it?

STEPH: Yes, that was fine, but the day after, his hamster died.

DEBRA: Oh no! What did you tell him?

STEPH: Well, I didn't want to tell him in the morning because he had a football match and I didn't want to upset him before that. Then, when he got home, his uncle had come round to take him out to buy a birthday present. So I didn't want to tell him then, because his uncle had just come over from America and it was a special occasion. We don't get to see him much and he wanted to take Kieran over to Toys 'R Us. But then it was getting later and later and I thought we can't tell him just before bedtime because he won't get to sleep. So I was trying to hint to my husband, 'John don't you think we should say something now?' Before we could do anything though, Kieran's gone up to his room and discovered that the cage is empty. So John sits him down and explains what has happened.

DEBRA: That must have been difficult.

STEPH: Well, it was all right, but then Kieran said he wanted to see the hamster. Well, sentimental old me, I'd just chucked it in the bin and I didn't want him to see that. So I got it out and it looked, well, a bit flat. So I thought, I can't just show it to him like that, I'll wrap it in a tissue. So I'm desperately trying to make this sort of shroud out of a tissue and I can hear them coming down the stairs. I'm trying to gesture to John, 'Not yet, not yet', but he got distracted by Kate who'd spilt her milk. So I have to show Kieran this sad-looking, squashed creature half-wrapped up in a coloured Kleenex and he asks me, 'Can we have a funeral?' So the next morning we place the hamster in a shoebox and dig a hole in the garden. And there we all are, standing around in the rain, then Kieran starts to cry and then John and I start to cry, so we're all standing around this bloody hamster's grave crying. It was quite moving really.

DEBRA: Aw, bless. How is he now?

STEPH: Well we asked him if he wanted another hamster and he said yes at first. But this morning he burst into my bedroom and said that he didn't want another one because if that one died he would feel just as bad. Then he said, 'It's very hard loving things, because they die and sometimes it's just too much.'

DEBRA: Well I suppose that's a lesson for life.

Finding Sense

Instead of applying themselves to coursework ahead of an imminent examination, Year Eleven pupils are arguing about the scene in the movie Finding Nemo *where Dory attempts to communicate with the whale.*

JENNA: She's not saying nothing! She's just going, whoooooowhaaaaaabooooooooooo and stuff.

EMMA: You are so wrong! She's saying words and everythin'.

JENNA: She so is not!

EMMA: She is, man! She's saying stuff like, Hallooooooooomeeesterwhale and stuff.

JENNA: She so isn't!

EMMA: Girl, you need to like listen better, you know? You're soooooooo stooooooopiiiiiiid.

Don't Go There

Colleagues have slightly veered off-task in a long meeting.

LIZ: I just know I'm going to end up calling Lois Dickman Lois Dickhead.

JENNY: Well it's perfectly apt. She is. It does exactly what it says on the tin as they say.

ROBERTA: You know, last year we'd arranged for our son to get some work experience back home in South Africa. But he kept putting off making the call to arrange things. I said, why don't you ring them? He says, Mum, I can't call someone whos name is Mr Wanker, I'll just crack up. Of course, it's actually Van Kerr, but you know kids.

LIZ: Oh poor lad, I think I'd have struggled with that one.

ROBERTA: That's nothing! The husband of a friend of mine had to give a speech and a presentation at this dinner. The woman they were there to honour was some important benefactor called Mrs Schetlippe...

LIZ: Oh no...

ROBERTA: Anyway, he was very worried about the speech and got all nervous about it. Of course, on the night he stands up and says, ladies and gentlemen, now we'd like to invite you all to give a huge thank-you to our benefactor, Mrs Shittylips.

Focking Americans!

A waiter brings pizzas to two American girls sitting in a trattoria by the side of the Strada Nova in Venice.

WAITER: There you go, ladies. Enjoy your meal!

BLONDE AMERICAN GIRL: Oh, er, grazie!

WAITER: Prego!

BRUNETTE AMERICAN GIRL: Er, signor! Scuzi.

WAITER: Yes, miss, how can I help you?

BRUNETTE AMERICAN GIRL: Like, this pizza's just *waaay* too big.

BLOND AMERICAN GIRL: Yeah. Like waaaaaay too big!

BRUNETTE AMERICAN GIRL: Could we like get a smaller one or something?

WAITER: You want smaller pizza?

BRUNETTE AMERICAN GIRL: Could we?

WAITER: Miss, this is a pizza-sized pizza. In Italy all pizzas should be this size. You wanna smaller pizza? Eat *half*!

He exits muttering.

WAITER: Focking Americans!

Bounced

Two pub bouncers stand a discreet two urinals apart in the gents.

BOUNCER 1: She said, I want you to make love to me in every room in this house.

BOUNCER 2: Blimey, what did you do?

BOUNCER 1: I went 'ome, didn't I?

BOUNCER 2: What? A munter, was she?

BOUNCER 1: No, it was a big house. Must have been seven rooms, plus the toilet.

BOUNCER 2: She didn't mean the toilet, surely?

BOUNCER 1: I dunno, I didn't wait to find out, did I?

Conditioning

Two mums talk at the school gates.

CHRISTINE: I put the big pram away yesterday!

GEMMA: Aww, was it very sad?

CHRISTINE: It was! I got all teary and then because I was booing, Emma got all upset.

GEMMA: Awwww, bless.

CHRISTINE: I had to give her Ben's old toy pushchair to cheer her up. Oh, *there's* a story. Daddy was not happy about Ben having his own pushchair. What's he want one of those for, he says?

GEMMA: Little whatsisname's got one!

CHRISTINE: They've all got them these days. I said, why shouldn't he have a pushchair, he's got a tea set and everything else? Well he's not 'aving a bleeding doll! And he wouldn't let him have a proper doll! So I got him a beany baby. Daddy's not happy about that. I said, oh well, if he turns out gay then it'll all be my fault, won't it? That tea set and the pushchair. Bound to do it, isn't it?

Cheese People

A harassed-looking supermarket worker attempts to manhandle a heavy trolley down an aisle only to find her way blocked by two larger trolleys full of assorted cheddars.

SUPERMARKET WORKER: Oh! Will those cheese people never learn!

As if!

A couple are watching a video of 'An American Werewolf in London' *with friends.*

GIRL: (snorting) Oh as if!

BOY: What?

GIRL: Well, as if the front window of a bus would break that easily!

BOY: O-kay.

A pause punctuated by the girl swatting the boy with a cushion.

BOY: Ow! What was that for?

GIRL: You.

BOY: (exasperated) What?

GIRL: You were being snide!

BOY: I said okay!

GIRL: You said it in a snidey way. You're pissed off because I criticised your film.

BOY: Well, for a start, it's not my film. I'm not pissed off, I was just surprised by what you said.

GIRL: Why?

BOY: (pausing video) Anita, for the last hour and a quarter or so, we've been watching a film about a man who gets bitten by a werewolf and turns into one himself, is haunted by his dead and decomposing best friend and dreams of Nazi pig creatures. But, almost at the end of the film the thing that you find impossible to believe is that a man could be thrown through the upstairs window of a crashing double-decker bus'. I just found it a bit surprising, all right?

Boy presses 'play' on the remote control.

GIRL: You're not remotely clever you know.

Chalk

A four year old finds daddy in the lounge.

ALICE: Daddy, I want to hear chalk.

DADDY: What's that, darling?

ALICE: I want to hear chalk please?

DADDY: I don't understand, darling.

ALICE: Please!

DADDY: That's very polite, darling, but I don't understand what you want.

ALICE: Please, please, please, Daddy!

DADDY: Darling, just tell me what it is you want I didn't understand you!

ALICE: (in tears) Please, I want to hear chalk, thank you!

DADDY: (exasperated) Argh! Darling, I want to help you but I don't understand what you want.

Mummy enters.

MUMMY: Oh dear, big tears! What's Daddy doing then?

DADDY: (irate) Fuck knows. She keeps saying she wants to hear chalk. I haven't got a fucking clue what she's talking about.

Mummy sighs and presses 'play' on the CD player. 'Venus as a Boy' begins to play.

MUMMY: Not 'chalk'...

DADDY: Bjork!

MUMMY: That's it! (to Alice) Daddy hasn't quite got the hang of this yet, has he?

Casanova on the 137

A young Casanova is chatting on his mobile while sitting on a bus.

CASANOVA: I am so glad you called, sweet. Yeaaaahh. Girl, I ain't sitting on no bus. I'm here driving, yeah? Yeah, well you see it soon, girl. You gonna come out with me tonight? Cooool. I'm sooo glad you called, yeah? I was thinking 'bout you... Let's meet up... Where? Okay, I'll take you there... Yeah, I'll take you there, girl. I won't bring my wheels if we're going there. That's all right. That's all right. I'll be there. What's your name, girl...? I know what your name is, girl, I want you to spell it. Donna. Dana! D-a-n-a, yeah? I knew that. I am sooo glad you called, yeah? I was thinking 'bout you.

Biting Jelly

At a cafe table mother and daughter and a moth-eaten toy monkey share a cappuccino and a muffin

LITTLE GIRL: (scrutinising the monkey) George has a jealous face.

MOTHER: Has he, darling? Why, is he jealous?

LITTLE GIRL: Because, he is jealous and he has a jealous face.

MOTHER: What does he look like with a jealous face?

LITTLE GIRL: (thinks for a while) Like he's biting jelly.

Dimensions

Two older men exchange pleasantries at a motorway service station in the north.

TED: How do, Will? Funny seeing you here! Where you off?

WILL: How do, Ted. I'm just off to see me mother like.

TED: Oh aye, how is she?

WILL: Not too good as it happens. She just got diagnosed with dimensions.

TED: Oooh, I'm sorry to hear that, Will.

WILL: You know, her age and all.

TED: Ooh, it's nasty that. I'm right sorry to hear it. You will give her my love, won't you?

WILL: I will, Ted, I will, thank you. Anyway, must be off.

TED: Right, well, I'll see you then Will.

Ted's missus arrives.

TED'S MISSUS: Who were that you were talking to?

TED: That were Will from t'Flowers.

TED'S MISSUS: Oh aye. How is he?

TED: Not so good, his old mum's just been diagnosed with dimensions.

TED'S MISSUS: She hasn't?

TED: She has.

TED'S MISSUS: Oooh, that's nasty.

Cannon Balls-up

A nervous schoolboy has been asked to read out loud in his history class.

SCHOOLBOY: ...though today scholars put much of Drake's success in countering the threat of the Armada down to the adverse weather conditions experienced by the Spanish rather than damage sustained from English cannon.

Thinking he's finished, the schoolboy waits for the next reader to begin.

Silence and a few muted sniggers.

TEACHER: I think the next reader is waiting for you to finish the sentence.

SCHOOLBOY: Sir?

TEACHER: If you look at where you finished reading you'll see that's not the end of the sentence. There's another word.

SCHOOLBOY (spots his omission)

Oh. Balls!

Class and teacher collapse.

SCHOOLBOY: What? *Oh!*

A Good Investment

An elderly gentleman buying an anniversary card in a shop.

WOMAN ASSISTANT: Ooh. Are you sure you want this card? It's very expensive. It's £3.98. Would you like to change it for another one?

GENTLEMAN: If that's the price, then that's the price. Anyway, look inside and see what it's for.

WOMAN ASSISTANT: Aaahh.

GENTLEMAN: I don't think £3.98 is too much for fifty years, do you? Some people look at us and they don't believe it, but it *can* last longer than a week. Not like now, when you marry some bugger and then you wake up and think, 'Oh I'm bored of him...or her.' No. £3.98 for fifty years . Sounds like a good investment to me.

No Great Shakes

In the early 1990s a train conductor approaches two revenue protection officers who are reading The Sun.

TRAIN CONDUCTOR: (pointing at a photograph) 'ere, who's he then?

TICKET EXAMINER: Home Secretary.

TRAIN CONDUCTOR: Oh.

There's a long pause.

TRAIN CONDUCTOR: I did 'im last night.

TICKET EXAMINER: Eh?

TRAIN CONDUCTOR: I did 'im. Penalty fare.

TICKET EXAMINER: You didn't!

TRAIN CONDUCTOR: Yeah I did. Didn't 'ave a ticket. He was going to Brighton.

TICKET EXAMINER: Probably going to their conference like.

TRAIN CONDUCTOR: (shrugs) Didn't 'ave a ticket. Couple of coppers with 'im I think. Says he doesn't need a ticket. News to me, I says. So I did 'im.

TICKET EXAMINER: What did he say?

TRAIN CONDUCTOR: Not much. His mate says, 'You've no idea who this is, have you?' I says no, who is he then? He says he's the Home Secretary. I mean, my other half's a secretary. No great shakes, is it?

110

Greek

A small publishing company in the south of England. The managing director emerges from his office to talk to an Editorial Assistant.

MD: Ah, Gayle. Regarding the interviews for the new staff writer. Sorry it took so long to read your notes on the interviews but I've been a bit pressed for time. Anyway, I've read them now and I'd like you to call in Theresa Harding for a second interview.

EDITORIAL ASSISTANT: Theresa Harding?

MD: That's right.

EDITORIAL ASSISTANT: The pretty one in the silk blouse?

MD: Was it silk? Anyway, if you could set that up ASAP, please?

EDITORIAL ASSISTANT: You want to interview her again?

MD: Yes, Gayle. Perfectly standard practice to ask a potential new employee in for a second interview. So if you wouldn't mind...

EDITORIAL ASSISTANT: I don't think you do, you know.

MD: Gayle... I've made a simple request, and I'd quite like you to carry out my wishes, if you don't mind.

EDITORIAL ASSISTANT: But she hasn't even got English Language GCSE.

MD: Gayle, not all gifted writers have to flow out of Oxbridge you know. I'm sure Tony Parsons never went anywhere like that.

EDITORIAL ASSISTANT: But she spelt Curriculum Vitae C.o.r.r.o.c.u.l.o.m V.e.t.a.e.

MD: Yes, well, if I'd wanted her to speak Greek I would have put that in the job description, wouldn't I? Now, get her in here!

Pity

Susanna is paying for drinks at a bar in rural Australia.

BARMAID: Excuse me, would you and your gentleman friend be interested in a free sausage sizzler?

SUSANNA: That's very kind of you, but, we're vegetarian.

BARMAID: Oh.

Pause.

BARMAID: (distraught) I'm sooo sorry!

Care in the Community

A community care worker and a trainee are visiting an old lady in her home in a northern steel town. The old lady is sat in a kitchen that was clearly once a cream colour. Above her head the ceiling has turned black from cigarette smoke.

CARE WORKER: (to trainee) Watch this. (to old lady)

Now then, love, do you get out much?

OLD LADY: Ooh no, I don't get out much.

CARE WORKER: Do you not?

OLD LADY: No.

CARE WORKER: No?

OLD LADY: Ooh no, I don't get out much.

CARE WORKER: Do you not?

OLD LADY: No.

OLD LADY: (pause) You know I don't get out much.

CARE WORKER: *No*! Do you not?

OLD LADY: I don't.

CARE WORKER: Oh.

Where You Hide Yourself

A female shopper has bumped into an acquaintance working in the homeware section of a well-known discount store.

SHOPPER: Oh, so this is where you hide yourself, is it? During the day?

SHOP WORKER: Oh yes, I'm always here, pricing things...

SHOPPER: Ooooh, I think I'd love your job!

SHOP WORKER: Oh aye?

SHOPPER: Oooh yes! Trouble is, I wouldn't be able to stop meself buying stuff.

Shop worker smiles as her acquaintance wanders off towards the chinoiserie.

SHOP WORKER: (to herself) Yeeeeees, *that's* how I ended up with that wok.

Offender Profile

A group of trainee store security guards are being shown the CCTV screens in a large high street store.

STORE DETECTIVE: Although this is a useful deterrent, and in some cases will provide the visual evidence needed to secure a conviction, it is no substitute for a store detective's eyes and experience. Although we are told to avoid stereotyping people, there are specific character traits you should look out for. Her, for example.

He points to a screen showing a middle-aged lady entering the store with a large bag.

STORE DETECTIVE: Classic offender profile: overweight, middle-aged, probably hormonal, isn't getting it from her husband any more, so she's taken to shoplifting for her thrills. See that big bag? Probably nothing in it, so she can squirrel away anything she takes a shine to. Probably stinks of piss too if she's anything like the usual offender. I think we'll call this type Mrs Hormonal unless any of you has a better suggestion?

A trainee lifts his hand.

STORE DETECTIVE: Go on then.

TRAINEE: I call her mum.

Unexpected Delivery

Colleague's chat at a workplace canteen table.

CAROL: Honestly, my Ian! He's such a scam merchant, do you know what he did once?

COLLEAGUE: Nah, go on.

CAROL: We had this newspaper delivery van we bought cheap from the local newsagent. We thought it would come in handy but didn't. So matey decides that he can do it up and sell it on. Course he's forgotten about the sliding door and the seat that faces out on the passenger side, so the deliverer can get in and out of the cab quicker. Anyway, he decides that it doesn't matter and that if anybody asks he's going to wing it, yeah? Anyway, he puts an ad in the paper and this guy phones up the same evening and asks to come and have a look. He's slapping it and rattling it, and opening it all up and everything, then he asks about the mileage and what the van's history is. Well, Ian didn't want him to know that it was a trade van, cos then you get half what you do for domestic use only, so thinking on his feet, he comes out with this cock and bull story about how I have terrible travel sickness and the only way we can get about is by turning the seat round so that I can just slide open the door and throw up whenever I needed to.

COLLEAGUE: He didn't! Cor! Did it work?

CAROL: Well, what do you think?

The Birthday Buddy

Daisy, six, is sat in the back of the car, half-listening to her mum and her mum's friend's conversation about birthday parties.

DAISY: I've got a friend whose birthday is the same day as mine!

FRIEND: Oooh.

MUM: Oh yes, you mean John? Yes, that means we'll never forget John's birthday then, will we?

DAISY: No.

Daisy's brow furrows.

DAISY: When is it?

Undersize Me

A mother approaches the counter at a famous fast-food franchise. No, not THAT one, the other one.

MOTHER: Can I have one small vanilla milkshake and a small chocolate one to go, please?

ASSISTANT: A milkshake, madam? Certainly. What flavour would you like?

MOTHER: One vanilla, one chocolate, please.

ASSISTANT: And what size?

MOTHER: Small.

ASSISTANT: So that's two milkshakes, one vanilla and one chocolate?

MOTHER: Yes please.

ASSISTANT: Right away, madam. But that will be two medium-sized milkshakes as we don't do small milkshakes.

MOTHER: I'm sorry?

ASSISTANT: The milkshakes will be medium-sized, because we don't do small-sized drinks at this company, just medium and large.

MOTHER: Er, okay...No, hang about! What do you mean, you only do medium and large? If there's only two choices then there isn't a medium choice, is there? Just small and large.

ASSISTANT: No, we don't do small, just medium and large.

MOTHER: But you can't! To have a medium you also have to have a small and large. You don't, so in fact all you are offering is two sizes, one of which is larger, one of which is smaller.

ASSISTANT: No, it's not small, it's medium.

MOTHER: Okay, whatever. Just give me the medium and forget it. (To woman in queue) Only a bloke could have come up with that idea.

Caffé Americano

A couple have just enjoyed a meal outside a restaurant in the Campo San Marina, Venice when they are approached by the waiter.

BERNICE: Mi scusi, signor. Uno cappuccino, uno espresso e uno piccollo Caffé Americano per favore.

WAITER: Ah, so *now* you speak Italian! Nothing for three courses and, now you want to speak it. Bueno.

BERNICE: I'm a little rusty.

WAITER: How can you not be rusty when you not try? So, you want a cappuccino, an espresso and a leetle Caffé Americano. You mean an espresso?

BERNICE: No, I just want a regular black coffee.

WAITER: (despairing) Madonna! Miss, you want a regular black coffee in Italy you ask for coffee, yes? Everybody knows what this is. You ask for Americano, you get a watered-down espresso. You ask for a leetle Caffé Americano you get a leetle brown water. Caffé Americano is only here for the Americans. American coffee is so bad is good only for washing feet.

Man's Other Best Friends

Dominic is recovering from a minor surgical procedure.

FRIEND: So you had a...erm

DOMINIC: Vasectomy, Uh-huh.

FRIEND: God, I can't even say it! Did it really hurt?

DOMINIC: Nah. I mean, there were brief periods of unpleasantness when the needle first went in, but the op itself doesn't hurt.

FRIEND: Were there nurses present?

DOMINIC: One. Actually, the pre-meds made her look like twins for a bit. She didn't point and make fun if that's what you mean.

FRIEND: So how do you feel now?

DOMINIC: It doesn't really hurt unless I overdo it. Can't walk very far though cos of the swelling.

FRIEND: I expect you're a bit bruised, aren't you?

DOMINIC: Bruised? When I look down it's like I've got Mike Tyson and Lennox Lewis french-kissing in my pants.

Objects of Desire

Little Molly has just taken her mum's instruction to put a cup down a little too literally, smashing it in the process.

MOLLY'S MUM: I'm so sorry!

KATIE'S MUM: Oh don't worry about it. It was just an orphan I let Katie play with sometimes. Kids are so literal at this age, aren't they?

MOLLY'S MUM: Oh I know, I'm constantly telling Molly to stop and not move then, in the same breath, telling her to put her jumper on or something. No wonder they're confused.

KATIE'S MUM: Well Katie has been a bit naughty at night of late. She wakes up, then finds any excuse she can to come and wake us up. So naturally we're getting a little grumpy about this. So I tell her that she's only allowed to come and wake mummy and daddy if it's something really, really important. Anyway, last night I get a little tug on my quilt and there's Katie, bawling her eyes out. So obviously I'm wide awake and wondering what on earth it is that upset her. So I say, 'Oh, love, what's the matter?' And she says, 'Mummy, I've got something really really important to tell you,' and she's blubbing, blubbing so much that I'm starting too. So I gather her up in the quilt and try and calm her down. Eventually she's calmed down enough so I can ask her what it is she wanted to ask me. She says, 'Mummy, I really, really want a pair of shiny shoes.' And she's off crying again.

MOLLY'S MUM: Noooooo! How do they ever survive until their teens?

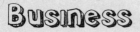

Business

A muralist is discussing a recent work-related annoyance.

MURALIST: Oh don't talk to me about the American customs people! I was working for this company that painted murals for rich clients. They'd asked me to go to New York to take measurements of a client's bedroom. The client wanted a special canvas panel with cherubs and stuff all over it. Anyway, I'm basically going to arrive in New York, go get the measurements and head back the same day, but as I'm going through US customs they ask me the usual, you know, whether the purpose of my visit is business or pleasure. Stupidly, I say business. Of course, I don't have the right paperwork for that so I have to go through this long, boring, and rather threatening, question and answer session where I describe exactly what I've been sent across the Atlantic to do. All the time that I'm trying to explain what it is I can feel one of the customs men getting more and more hostile until at last he blurts out, 'You came here to measure a god damn ceiling? Are you trying to tell me that we don't have a single goddamn person in the entire United States of America capable of measuring a ceiling?' I didn't have the heart or the courage to tell him that the only reason I was there was because his countrymen had fucked up the measuring... *twice*.

Scaring the Extras

A movie insider repeats a third-hand story about the making of a Scottish historical epic.

COPY-TAKER: My mate says they had to stop filming for a day because he insisted on wearing his kilt in the traditional Scottish way, if you know what I mean. So he was doing his first scene, running across the heather, and his knob keeps peeking out of the bottom of the kilt. They tried a couple of takes, but it was scaring the extras, so they had to get the costumier to run up another, longer, kilt for him.

A Mother's Lament

A middle-aged mum strides briskly across the supermarket pushing a baby in a trolley and dragging another child in her wake in response to a customer announcement about a little boy found sobbing in the soup aisle.

MUM: (sighing) When did we become the Tannoy family?

A Really Swish Showhome

A builder and his interior designer are at lunch with journalists.

BUILDER: We had this development in East Sussex, and everything on site had sold well so we hadn't bothered with a showhome. Then, as happens, one of the houses came back on the market, and because it was the last one on sale—

INTERIOR DESIGNER: It was a gorgeous house. Absolutely nothing wrong with it.

BUILDER: Exactly. Nothing wrong with it at all, but the perception is that the last one on the shelf must be a bit iffy. So I thought, I know, we'll turn this one into a really swish showhome, I mean, really deck it out and include all the styling features and furniture in the house price. Site manager thought I was mad, but it was getting near year-end and I just wanted the house sold.

INTERIOR DESIGNER: He told us to really go for it, so we did. We did it really contemporary; shiny metal, purple curtains, lots of designer names.

BUILDER: I mean, to me, it looked like a tart's boudoir, and the site manager gave me some real stick over it, but you know, it looked swish enough if you like that sort of thing. And it bloody cost us a packet.

INTERIOR DESIGNER: We spent nearly £10,000 on it, so you can imagine.

BUILDER: Anyway, just two days after we unveil the showhome I get a call from the site manager saying the house is sold and would I like to come down and meet the buyer. Of course, I'm dead chuffed it's sold and want to rub it in to the site manager cos of all the stick I've taken, so I pop down there and he introduces me to the bloke who's bought it. Anyway, I'm just about to ask him what he thought of the interior design job, when his bloody guide dog barks.

Glee Club

Two young mothers sit on a town centre bench smoking and watching as their kids chase pigeons.

MOTHER 1: I just don't know how I get through the day, I really don't.

MOTHER 2: At least when you're asleep it all goes away for a bit.

MOTHER 1: Yeah, I know what you mean.

MOTHER 2: Still, you 'ave to go on, don't you?

MOTHER 1: Yeah, you 'ave to soldier through it.

Brazil Nuts

Dad is relating a story that should have waited until after dinner.

DAD: Your Uncle Evan is friends with this bloke who used to work with old people in the community. Around Christmas he'd have to go and visit them in their houses and make sure they were all right for the holiday. The old biddies used to love giving him little Christmas presents, you know, talc from Wilco, monogrammed handkerchiefs – that kind of stuff. Then one day, he went to see this old girl, not one of his regulars, and she offers him this bag of brazil nuts that she's been given. She can't eat them because of her teeth. He's a veggie and he was going to pick some up anyway for the nut roast so he says, 'Thank you very much.' Anyway, Christmas comes and goes and they end up using up all the nuts. When he goes back to work he drops in to see the old girl again to see how she is. When he gets there she's slurping away at an orange with her false teeth balanced on the chair arm next to her. He thanks her for the nuts and she waves it away saying, 'Don't worry, love, I was just glad to see they didn't go to waste. Once I'd sucked the chocolate off I didn't know what to do with them.

DAUGHTER: Urgh!

DAD: It gets worse the more you think about it.

Trouble with Snails

A representative of a house building company has just been asked about environmental problems with a new site.

CEO: (spluttering) Environmentalists! Don't talk to me about envirobloodymentalists! One hundred million pounds this site is going to generate and what's stopping us breaking ground? A snail. No, a twin-lipped snail. This is one of the only places it's been found in the bastard country and we've got a bloody colony of the slimy little shits. I mean, have you ever heard of one? What the bloody hell does it need another set of lips for anyway? I mean, would you miss the twin-lipped snail if it got wiped out tomorrow? I know I wouldn't! Bloody environmentalists. You'd think they'd have something more important to do.

Tough Love

A mum is in a queue at the grocers with her young daughter when the old lady in front leans back in her motorised buggy and smiles fondly.

OLD LADY: How old is she?

MUM: Just turned seven.

OLD LADY: Awww, just turned seven. My little grandson is six next week. Eeeh, I can't believe how quick it's gone! The older one, Laurence, he'll be *ten* this year!

MUM : I know! My little boy will be five in May.

OLD LADY: Oh he's a May baby, just like me! Is *he* a typical Sagittarian?

MUM : Erm, ooh, I don't know. What's typical?

OLD LADY: Hee-heee-heeee. Stubborn. Very stubborn. Just like my grandson. Ooh, he's a real little boy. Always on the go. I love it! Not like the *other* one. He's very quiet... *Studious*... I say, Laurence, you need to toughen up! It's a hard life out there! Mmm... he's a bit of a wuss really.

The 'Flight of the Valkyries' suddenly blares out from a bag in the buggy's basket.

OLD LADY: (reaching for her bag) Oh, that'll be for me!

The Tourists

A husband and wife relate their latest overseas adventure.

WIFE: Oh yes, it was an exceptional experience wasn't it, darling?

HUSBAND: Yes, very interesting.

WIFE: We didn't spend much time in Harare, but the estate we stayed on was very comfortable. Of course the sun was very welcome. We had trips to the wildlife park in Gweru. Rode on an elephant...

HUSBAND: The lions.

WIFE: Yes, we saw the lions actually hunting, which our guide said was very unusual. The National Park outside Bulawayo was just stunning. We saw leopard cubs there in the evening didn't we, darling?

HUSBAND: Yes, in the evening.

WIFE: Again, our guide informed us this was very, *very* rare.

HUSBAND: *Very* rare apparently.

WIFE: Yes *very* rare. The day after, we took a helicopter ride over Victoria Falls, then in the evening we had a lovely sunset cruise on the Zambezi.

HUSBAND: The way the water creates a rainbow as it goes over the falls is most spectacular.

WIFE: Oh yes, a real wonder. But I'm afraid things took bit of a dive then, didn't they, dear?

HUSBAND: Yes, kind of spoiled things really.

WIFE: Yes, the restaurant...

HUSBAND: The fish...

WIFE: Yes the fish was rather dry.

HUSBAND: Very disappointing.

WIFE: Yes, *very*.

Boys Will Be...

Kate is walking home from school with her twin boys and chatting to a neighbour.

KATE: So I go in the garden and there they are again. At it like cat and dog they were. They're shouting and pushing each other around so you break 'em up and tell 'em not to be so bleedin' nasty. Then you turn your back and they're at it again, this time they're punching, kicking, biting, spitting. Honestly! It took four of us to pull them apart, silly little boys! I mean, it's just not the kind of behaviour you expect from two forty year olds, is it?

The Naturalist's Needs

A TV presenter/naturalist is shopping for a laptop on Tottenham Court Road.

TV PRESENTER: The software package is fine, but I'm a little concerned about the chassis.

SHOP ASSISTANT: I can assure you it's quite hardy, sir.

TV PRESENTER: Yeah, well where I'm going, hardy doesn't really cut it.

SHOP ASSISTANT: I am assured its very strong, sir.

TV PRESENTER: It's plastic though, isn't it?

SHOP ASSISTANT: Aluminium casing coated in plastic, sir. So it's very light.

TV PRESENTER: Light is fine, but I need it to be really tough.

SHOP ASSISTANT: I assure you, sir, this machine is tough, durable and reliable and can take anything you can throw at it.

TV PRESENTER: You're sure about that? I mean, I love it and everything, but if its not tough...

SHOP ASSISTANT: May I enquire where sir will most likely be using his laptop?

TV PRESENTER: Quite varied terrain. Some desert, some equatorial rainforest, perhaps arctic conditions too.

SHOP ASSISTANT: Well then, this machine is perfectly adaptable to extremes of temperature, plus you could drop it from a considerable height onto bare rock and it would be fine. As I said before, I am quite certain that this laptop can take any punishment that you throw at it.

TV PRESENTER: Yes, but that's what they said about my last one.

SHOP ASSISTANT: And may I enquire what accident befell that particular instrument, sir?

TV PRESENTER: A rhinoceros sat on it.

Pause.

SHOP ASSISTANT: On reflection, perhaps sir would prefer to try out one of these titanium-shell products.

A Higher Power

*A meeting of Alcoholics Anonymous in south-west London.
A Glaswegian with a very broad accent has been sharing,
uninterrupted, for the last half-hour.*

GLASWEGIAN: I mean, I don't hold it against them, do you
know what I mean? I mean, it's horrible what they went
through, do you know what I mean? But to put that on your
own kin, well, do you know what I mean...? I mean, it's not
right, is it? Do you know what I mean?

A scraping of chairs and a female AA member rises to her feet.

AA MEMBER: Look, I'm sorry, but no, I don't know what you
mean! And I swear I will drink again if I have to listen to one
more word of what you're saying!

She exits noisily. There is a very uncomfortable silence.

GLASWEGIAN: You know, I think that was very brave of her,
do you know what I mean?

Boing!

An instructor on a course for railway revenue protection officers is bracing his students for the rigours ahead.

INSTRUCTOR: Normally we encourage all of you to say good morning to the passengers as they leave the train. However, if you've had a bad morning you'll find that if you say, 'Fuck you, sir' very quickly, it sounds just like 'thank you, sir' to the passengers pushing past you. My old gaffer always told me that if I wanted to confuse people then, instead of saying 'morning', say 'Boing' – all cheerful like. Vary the way you say it and no one is any the wiser. Brightens up the day in between the scrotes and the junkies anyway.

Too Much Information

A gentlemen's public convenience in Hammersmith. A large young man with a deep basso profundo voice enters a cubicle. Not long after, a mobile phone ring tone can be heard from his cubicle.

YOUNG MAN: Yeah? Nah. Nah, I can't... Nah, I can't... Am on the toilit. Nah, am on the toilit. Yeah. Yeah am on the toilet... doing a shit.

What sounds like a huge number of people on the other side of the telephone conversation begin to laugh hysterically. Then the men occupying the cubicles to either side of the young man begin to join in.

YOUNG MAN: Wha'? (Getting it) Ur. Urrr!
Ahuhahuhahuhahuhahuh....

There!

Two young women are going home on a night bus.

BLONDE: You know...*there*.

BRUNETTE: *Where* there?

BLONDE: *There* there.

BRUNETTE: Eh?

BLONDE: Think about it.

BRUNETTE: Look, just tell me will you?

BLONDE: (indicating her crotch) *There* there.

BRUNETTE: Oh *there*!

BLONDE: At last!

BRUNETTE: (pondering for a moment) Karen?

BLONDE: Hmmm?

BRUNETTE: How did you get a splinter *there*?

Salt of the Earth to Planet Boyfriend

Northerner Rachel is sat at her desk in the offices of a television company leafing through a department store flyer. She presses a programmed number on her phone and turns on the speaker.

BOYFRIEND: 'Ullo?

RACHEL: 'Ullo, lover, it's me.

BOYFRIEND: Oh 'ullo.

RACHEL: Just got up?

BOYFRIEND: Uh.

RACHEL: Alright for some! Eh, Army and Navy have got a sale on.

BOYFRIEND: Eh?

RACHEL: It's like Allders or Rackhams. They've got beds in t'sale. We should get one.

BOYFRIEND: What? Like kid's beds?

RACHEL: No, proper grown-up sized beds.

BOYFRIEND: I don't want a bed with a chuffin' sail on it.

RACHEL: You what?

BOYFRIEND: I mean, is it boat-shaped and stuff?

RACHEL: What you talking about now?

BOYFRIEND: You said bed's got a sail. Is it boat-shaped?

RACHEL: No! Oooh, what are you like? I said beds in t'sale! Int' shop!

BOYFRIEND: What shop?

RACHEL: Army and Navy!

BOYFRIEND: Is that a shop?

RACHEL: Yes! Like Rackhams!

BOYFRIEND: I thought tha' you said navy bed'd got a sail. I don't want to sleep in a novelty bed.

RACHEL: Bloo-dee-hell! Go away, I'll talk to you later, when you've woken up! (disconnects) What chuffin' planet is 'e on?

The Important Stuff

A mother is travelling on a London to Brighton train with her two young boys. The train is paused in a station when the younger boy sits up and points excitedly through the window.

BOY: Look!

The mother follows the direction of the boy's pointed finger to a huge poster promoting 'Days Away by Rail' where lots of people are doing all manner of exciting seaside activities.

MOTHER: Hmm. The chance of a lifetime?

The boy looks witheringly at his mother.

BOY: Nooooo. *Ice cream!*

A Traveller's Tale

Kirsten and Steve are just back from India.

KIRSTEN: Just before we went we asked everyone we knew who'd been before what to look out for, and they all, to a man...

STEVE: And a woman.

KIRSTEN: ...said, you're going to get the shits. Totally unavoidable.

STEVE: My mate who's travelled quite a bit says it's best to get it over with while you're in a big city with some decent plumbing. So while you're in Delhi, just lick the pavement.

CHLOE: Lick the pavement? Urgh!

STEVE: He swore blind that it worked every time. Trouble is, when you get to Delhi you can't see the pavement because of all the thousands of people crammed on to it. So it takes me for ever, but at last I find this relatively clear stretch of pavement and I bend down and lick it.

KIRSTEN: He licked it!

STEVE: I gave it a good old slurp, and thought 'bring it on!'

KIRSTEN: Then there's this anguished cry from behind us...

STEVE: And there's this old bloke steaming towards us with a broom in his hand. 'I just cleaned that!' he yells. So we legged it.

CHLOE: But did it work?

KIRSTEN: Oh yeah, it worked all right. But not for another five days. On a crowded train halfway to Bombay.

STEVE: I had to throw my shorts and kecks off the train and wrap K's shawl around me.

KIRSTEN: Yeah, I won't be travelling with Steve again.

Come Together

Gay dad is discussing another possible addition to the family.

GAY DAD: So we've been talking about it, and talking about it and, to be honest, I'm still not sure. I mean, it could be lovely, but I'm forty for god's sake! Do I need to do this again? And Jessica...

FRIEND: Is that mummy one?

GAY DAD: No, that's mummy two. Jessica is convinced it's going to happen. Anyway, she comes up to me while I'm drying the coffee cups and says, 'Hey, Ben, if we do have another baby it will be just your sperm or Jamie's sperm, won't it? I mean, you won't mix it together or anything?' And I'm like, God woman! What do you think we'd do? Just collect some that we had lying around the bedroom or something?

Catch 23

Amelia, six, has been watching The Incredibles *on DVD.*
Suddenly she rushes into the kitchen red-faced and anxious.

AMELIA: Mummy, Mrs Incredible used a swear word!

MUMMY: I don't think she did, lovey. This is a film for
children and they're very careful about those sorts of things.

AMELIA: She *did*, Mummy, I heard it!

MUMMY: Well I think you might have misheard something…

AMELIA: No! She said a rude word!

MUMMY: What do think she said?

AMELIA: Mummy, I can't tell you because I'm not *allowed* to
say rude words!

Andy's Do

Two female office workers have met for lunch in a shopping mall cafe. One is wearing glasses and is sporting a large plaster on her chin.

2: Eh, I haven't seen you in glasses for yonks! What happened to your contacts?

1: Lost one at Andy's do, didn't I?

2: Oh. What you done to your face?

1: Carpet burn.

2: No!

1: 'tis.

2: Dirty mare! This at Andy's do?

1: Yeah...Wouldn't have minded but I was only crawling around looking for me contact lens and whoosh!

2: He never!

1: He did. I didn't have heart to stop him by that stage. You know his dog died, don't you?

2: I didn't, no. Aw, bless!

Another Woman

*An Italian grandmother, a first-generation immigrant, sits in a
play park watching her three grandchildren and, fighting back
tears, as she talks to a complete stranger.*

GRANDMOTHER: Oh my god! It's too much for me. Three
children! I'm worn out! Three weeks ago my daughter dump
them on me. For three weeks now, I hear nothing from her.
She come up from Brighton. She dump the kids and she go.
Since then, nothing. These kids have missed three weeks of
school. They're getting no education! I do my best but I am
worn out. I bring them to park, I feed them, but look at them.
Energy, energy. Today I go into social. Three weeks ago my
daughter dumped these kids. I've got no help. No one knows a
thing. I've been on the phone, and it's all mouth. Nothing has
happened. I never ask for anything in my life, now there's
nothing. I am seventy years old! My husband has heart
condition. He takes so many pills... oh my god... I've got four
babies at home. I can't do it!

She gets up off the bench.

GRANDMOTHER: I must go keep an eye on them. I hope
you don't mind me telling you this but you're, you know,
another woman, yes?

Memories

Two old friends block the entrance to a department store.

FRIEND 1: I know it sounds daft, but although I've not seen you for a long time it doesn't feel like a long time. Do you know what I mean?

FRIEND 2: I do yes.

FRIEND 1: You're not with your partner any more are you?

FRIEND 2: Oh yes.

FRIEND 1: Twickenham, wasn't it?

FRIEND 2: Kingston.

FRIEND 1: That's right! You 'ad a dog!

FRIENDS 2: A cat. Smokey.

FRIEND 1: That's right, a cat! Snowy, wasn't it?

FRIENDS 2: Smokey.

FRIEND 1: Ooh, I remember it like it were yesterday!

Americans in London

An American woman and her teenage son are riding the Bakerloo Line.

SON: Mom?

WOMAN: Yes, sugar?

SON: Is Waterloo station like where they fought the battle?

WOMAN: Oh, er sure, I guess it must be, honey.

SON: So, underneath the station there could be bows and arrows and spears and stuff? You know, in the ground?

WOMAN: I bet there is, honey.

SON: Cool!

Meat

Young women have been discussing first loves.

KATE: I dumped him.

SARAH: Aw. Why?

KATE: (sighing) Because we were having one of those post-sex confession conversations where you feel comfortable enough to talk about what you used to do with your previous partners. Well, I fess up to once having a threesome with a boyfriend and his mate. Sonny Jim admits that when he worked in a butcher's shop he used to fuck slabs of meat.

SARAH: Urghh!

KATE: And *that's* why I'm veggie.

Bliss

Two lady haberdashers chat as they arrange the autumn window display.

HABERDASHER 1: Oh, have you got your *new* boots on?

(Haberdasher 2's eyes all but roll back into her head with pleasure).

HABERDASHER 2: Oh yes!

HABERDASHER 1: And?

HABERDASHER 2: Oh they're *bliss*! Honest, it's like wearing slippers. I bought meself another pair, just in case.

HABERDASHER 1: Just in case of what?

HABERDASHER 2: (breathily) Oh, just in case.

Microcosm

A tired-looking mother stands hands on hips in the play park, watching her two young children tumble in the dirt.

MOTHER: (shouting) Jordan! Syria! Play nice!

Enough Underwear

Michael has just returned from a visit to his parents and is debriefed by his flatmates.

MICHAEL: Oh god, it's good to be back in the smoke!

FLATMATE 1: How are the folks?

MICHAEL: Fine. Dad's getting into retirement. But honestly, you can tell they've not seen anybody in a while.

FLATMATE 2: I get my leg talked off the minute I walk through the door back home too.

MICHAEL: Well mine always used to talk in stereo but now they're chatting away about two different things. Mum wants me to know all about the problems with the guttering and Dad wants to tell me what he thought about the Turner Prize. And they're both making total eye contact all the time so it's not as if you can phase one out for a bit.

FLATMATE 1: Aw, it's sweet really. They're obviously pleased to see you

MICHAEL: It is sweet. You know, love 'em dearly, but that wartime generation get weirder the older they get. On the few occasions when I've got just Mum talking at me, Dad will be in the kitchen washing up and he farts really loud about every couple of minutes, and I've got to keep a straight face while Mum's telling me about someone's cancer operation.

FLATEMATE 2: At least he doesn't blame it on the cat. My Dad does.

MICHAEL: Then, when Mum's out making the hundredth cup of tea that hour, Dad's talking about what a difficult decision it was to take early retirement. I mean, that's actually interesting and I'm keen to know what their plans are and everything. After all, Dad always wanted to go on a foreign trip and once he retired. And then he says, 'Well, we've budgeted as best we can, son. We've stocked up on stuff too. Both your Mum and I have stocked up on enough socks and underwear and stuff to keep us going until, well, *you know*.' I mean, what the fuck does that mean? Enough underwear until *you know*. He's sixty! How on earth can you know how much underwear you're going to need until you *you know*?!

Bad Medicine

A sweet, grey-haired old lady is talking to the receptionist at her local doctor's surgery.

OLD LADY: Well I take them. I *do* take them. Cos that's what Dr Morgan tells me to do. So I do take them. I mean, I'm not one to question. But you see, I take them and they make me ill. I mean, if I have to be ill, then I have to be ill. So be it. But I don't think they should be making me ill, love, do you? I mean, I'm not one to cause a fuss or anything but if you ask me there's been a bit of a fucking cock-up, if you'll pardon my French.

Bacteria

An older woman approaches the shop assistant in a health food store with a bio-yoghurt from the cool cabinet.

WOMAN: 'Scuse me, can you tell me what this has got innit please?

ASSISTANT: Well, that one's got bacteria in it.

WOMAN: What's that then?

ASSISTANT: Well it's like bacteria... Erm, it like ferments and it's healthy for you.

WOMAN: (grimacing) I'm not sure I want bacteria in me.

ASSISTANT: Oh no, it's very good for you!

WOMAN: I don't think so.

The woman hands the assistant the yoghurt and all but runs out of the shop.

Into the Wild

Two shelf-stackers are discussing the forthcoming holiday season.

A: So that's it then, eh? Four o'clock and you're off, eh?

B: Yeah, that's me. Can't wait.

A: Off on your toes, eh?

B: Yup.

A: Once more into the wild blue yonder? Horizons new?

B: Yeah 'sright.

A: Just waiting for four o' clock and that's it. Whoosh!

B: Yeah, that's me, whoosh!

A: Holiday of a lifetime.

B: Hoping so.

A: Cool. So where is it you're going again?

B: Centre Parcs.

A: Yeah?

B: Yeah.

A: Cool!

Guántanamo

Two dads are helping their young children around the equipment in a play park. The first dad, who wears a flamboyant, wide-brimmed leather hat, speaks in hushed tones about a recent trip to America while his friend nods grimly.

MAN IN HAT: I mean, I know with Iraq, Afghanistan, Guántanamo they've got to do what they've got to do. Y'know, I understand that. 'Sdifferent times. I understand that. But y'know, at JFK... you just don't expect that kind of treatment.

FRIEND: (adopts US accent) It's a matter of National Securiteeeee.

MAN IN HAT: But I mean, who do you complain to, y'know? I mean, they call someone, you talk to them and it's all 'e's just doing 'is job, sir. I mean, maybe I *should* get a new passport. But y'know, why should I? I've *worked* there. I've worked *everywhere*. It doesn't make me *one of them* does it? 'Snot right.

FRIEND: (snorts) I wouldn't go to America. Not if you paid me. You know what I call Americans, don't ya?, *Humourless, redneck, reeeeetards!*

The man in the hat gulps and regards his friend as though seeing him properly for the very first time.

MAN IN THE HAT: Well, you know, I suppose they've got to do what they've got to do.

The Stuff of Dreams

A manager is gathering staff together for a meeting.

MANAGER: Hi, Paula, are you about ready?

PAULA: Just printing off the reports.

MANAGER: Fab! Kirsty? Are you all set?

KIRSTY: Oh hello. You know, I had a dream about you last night.

MANAGER: Oh yes? Let me guess, you were throwing bricks at me or something.

KIRSTY: Oh no, quite the contrary actually.

MANAGER: Oh, er, ha ha ha ha ha.

KIRSTY: Yes, I woke up quite drained.

MANAGER: So, if we're just waiting for Paula...

KIRSTY: We were in your new house too. I don't remember your lady being there though.

MANAGER: Ha ha ha ha ha!

KIRSTY: You've still got that emerald green chenille bedspread, haven't you? The one in the estate agent's details?

MANAGER: Ha ha ha ha ha ha ha ha ha... Anyway...

KIRSTY: Yes, I have to say I'm looking at you in an entirely different light this morning.

PAULA: All done!

MANAGER: Fan-tastic. Okay, er meeting room five, is it? Oh, I've forgotten whose turn it is to do coffee?

KIRSTY: It's alright, darling, I'll get it. I should think you need the rest.

MANAGER: Ha ha ha ha ha ha ha.

Guests

Tom is having his son's school friends over to tea, one of whom is the local rich kid. The rich kid completes his investigative circuit of the two-bedroom first floor flat and sniffs.

RICH KID: Where's the rest of your house?

Later, Tom discovers a different boy staring up at one of his pieces of original art.

BOY: What's that?

TOM: It's a canvas with a painting on it.

BOY: What's it for?

TOM: Decoration.

BOY: (sneering) Oh.

Cool

Two young white men in baseball caps, chunky jewellery and very low-slung jogging bottoms shuffle unsteadily towards a corner shop in a Bedfordshire suburb.

1: Aw, man, you should see my new wheels, man!

2: Yeah, man whatcha got yeah?

1: Renaul Megan, man.

2: Cool.

1: Yeah, I mean, it's not hot or nothing, you know?

2: No, man, it's cool.

1: Nah, man, I mean, it's not like *hot*, y'know?

2: Nah, man Megan's is cool. Ma bro, got one, yeah?

1: Nah, nah, nah, man, you're not feelin' me right. I mean, it ain't *hot*, y'know. It ain't, y'know, *hot*.

2: (uncertainly) Nah, I'm feelin you, man, yeah?

Both men take a step out into the road towards the shop causing a grey-haired old lady in her car to brake suddenly.

As the men stop, one man's jogging bottoms slip down to his ankles causing the old lady to put her hand to her mouth and titter loudly.

As he retrieves his trousers he exchanges a nonplussed look with his friend.

1 and 2: *Wha—?*

A Simple Truth

In the kids department of a popular fashion retailer, Mum pulls a pretty dress from a rack and holds it up against her daughter. She looks thoughtful for a second, then slips the dress off the hanger.

MUM: Look can you just try this on, darling?

DAUGHTER: Oh, Mummy!

MUM: Come on, give me your coat!

The daughter slips into the dress with some effort.

MUM: Hmmm. I'm not sure. I think it makes your tummy stick out.

DAUGHTER: (proudly) No, Mummy, my tummy sticks out anyway! The dress doesn't make it do it!

A Cracking Bit of Cheese

A barber's shop in Surrey and a young woman of Mediterranean descent is cutting a middle-aged man's hair.

WOMAN: You know, I thought I'd be faithful to Cheshire for ever, but I had some Port Salut the other day.

MAN: Ooh, that's a cracking bit of cheese that is. Creamy...

WOMAN: And mild, isn't it? Oh yes, I have to say I'm a different woman after trying that.

MAN: Well, if it's mild you want, you can't beat a bit of buffalo mozzarella for my money.

WOMAN: My boyfriend swears by it, but I've never been tempted myself. I still remember that horrible French one.

MAN: Camembert?

WOMAN: (dry retching) Ugh, yes. You know, I just don't think foreigners can do cheese. Know what I mean?

MAN: I do, love. Stick to what you know, that's what I say.

WOMAN: Cheshire every time for me then... Sorry, I can't remember, did you say you wanted this over or around your ears?

Haggling

A small boy approaches a home-made cake stand at a busy craft market.

SMALL BOY: How much is that chocolate cake, then?

STALL GIRL: Go on, haggle with me. Tell me how pretty I am and I'll let you have it for 50p.

SMALL BOY: (horrified) 50p?!

Boy runs off in disgust.

STALL GIRL: Charming!

The Inheritance

An old woman, her middle-aged son and an exceedingly elderly dog wait in a south London Veterinary Surgery. The old woman hands her son a newspaper clipping.

OLD WOMAN: See, this is what I was talking about.

SON: It's a paper shredder. What do you want with a paper shredder?

OLD WOMAN: But don't you think it's a good price?

SON: Yes, I suppose so, but why do you need one?

OLD WOMAN: Well I have so much stuff to get rid of. So many pieces of paper.

SON: Why don't you put it in the recycling bin, Mum. That's what I would do!

OLD WOMAN: I couldn't do that. People might read it!

SON: What do you have on paper that's so private and important?

OLD WOMAN: That's not the point! I just don't want people to know things about me when I'm dead. Anyway, it's something for you to inherit.

SON: Can't you just buy a Mercedes?

A Generous Helping

At the shopping mall two rather well-proportioned ladies waddle out of the ladies loos and head for the downward escalators.

LADY: (pointing over towards an eatery)

I think we should go back there again for lunch. They 'ad really big jacket potatoes when I went in last time. And you could 'ave *two* fillings! Beans, coleslaw, cheese... I 'ad coleslaw last time and they said oh you can 'ave another if you like and I thought oh, all right. Bit of a funny combination though... Oh! Or you can have tuna!

Sniffs.

LADY: But I'm not *really* a tuna person.

The Suspect

Two men are talking about pets on a train stalled between London and Norwich.

MAN 1: Don't talk to me about tropical fish! I've 'ad nothing but grief with tropical fish.

MAN 2: Why's that, then?

MAN 1: Well, first lot I 'ad, 'andsome tank, loads of fish in it. Cost a bomb but kids love it. Know what I mean?

MAN 2: Yeah.

MAN 1: Yeah well, went on holiday, didn't I? Set up these drip feeders and everything. Spent ages making sure they were going to be alright while I was away. Came back. Fackin' thermostat thingy's up the spout. Fish boiled.

MAN 2: Fack.

MAN 1: Fackin' right. Ones that ain't boiled made a jump for it, and they're all rotten on the carpet, ain't they?

MAN 2: Fackin' 'ell.

MAN 1: I 'ad loads. Should 'a' cost a packet but I got a deal, yeah? Bloke says he'll throw in this dwarf piranha. I thought, I'm 'aving that! Piranha, mate! Don't see too many of them in a tank.

MAN 2: 'Strue, mate.

MAN 1: So I pops him in. Little fella like. Not much bigger than a guppy. Next morning, there's one o' me terras floating with 'is tail bit off.

MAN 2: No!

MAN 1: 'Sright. I think, 'allo. Bet I know who's to blame for this, Mr Piranha.

MAN 2: They're known for it, ain't they?

MAN 1: Well there's a lot of rubbish talked...

MAN 2: Oh yeah!

MAN 1: Anyway. Next day, same story. Siamese fightin' fish floating on 'is back, no tail. Now I'm pretty sure who's to blame. Day after that, the guppy. Day after that, me barb's gone. Next day, all me fucking swordtails have gone. Got to be the piranha, ain't it?

MAN 2: Fack, mate!

MAN 1: Anyway, this keeps on till there's just this one ropey-looking angel fish and me piranha left. Wake up next morning. Piranha, dead. Tail bitten off. Just the angel fish left.

MAN 2: Fack, man, who'd 'a' thought it, eh?

MAN 1: I'm telling you, mate. To this day I don't understand how that piranha managed to bite it's own fackin' tail off.

The Actor Who Couldn't

An assistant stage manager is discussing her last tour of duty at Glyndebourne.

STAGE MANAGER: So the director has spent two whole weeks of day-in, day-out rehearsal explaining to the guy playing the lead that, at the end of the opera, his character has to strain to wrench open the door, beyond which he will enter a state of wisdom and enlightenment. It's supposed to be a real trial of strength for him to open the door, but every time the actor gets to that scene he flings it open like it's just a piece of thin plywood which, of course, it is. Anyway, no matter how many times the director explains the scene to him, the actor just isn't getting it. Eventually, for the performances, we had to get one of our beefiest assistant stage managers and tie him to the back of the door with two other blokes hanging onto it, just to stop this idiot flinging it open and ruining the scene.

Teutonic Plates

On a train into London a rather excitable man has been reading the cover of a newspaper clearly raised by the woman opposite to exclude him.

MAN: Aw, there's been an earthquake. Look! An earthquake... aw. Do you know what happens when there's an earthquake? Do you? Do you know what happens when there's an earthquake?

Woman smiles weakly.

MAN: It's all right, I know, I'll tell you. You see, underneath the world there's these big teutonic plates and these plates slip and slide around and WHAM!

(Claps loudly.)

MAN: They crash into each other. CRASH! Just like that. And there's one in Los Angeles and there's one in the sea near Portugal. CRASH! Just like that they go. Did you know that? I knew that!

The woman smiles in as friendly a way as she can muster and turns the page of her newspaper. The man squints at the new page of the newspaper for a moment and then his eyes light up with glee.

MAN: Look! There's been a tornado! Do you know what happens when there's a tornado? Do you? I know! I can tell you if you want...

A Song for Pyewacket

Next door's cat is in season, and this has attracted a whole posse of feline admirers, all eager to serenade her.

ANYA: (three and a bit years old) Mummy? What's that noise?

MUMMY: That's the cats next door darling.

ANYA: What are they doing, Mummy?

MUMMY: Erm, they're singing, darling.

ANYA: (harrumphs loudly) They're not very good!

Tara's Terror

A young woman and her neighbour are chatting in a local post office queue.

CHLOE: Oh god, I feel awful! I must look a real state!

NEIGHBOUR: Well, I didn't want to say, but you *do* look tired, love.

CHLOE: Night from hell last night.

NEIGHBOUR: Had a good time, did you?

CHLOE: Tara got run over.

NEIGHBOUR: No! Oh I'm sorry I thought...

CHLOE: Quarter past seven.

NEIGHBOUR: Oh poor little mite, what happened?

CHLOE: She was playing with her football in the front garden. Anyway, she must have scooped it over the fence...

NEIGHBOUR: Oh no!

CHLOE: ...ran into the road after it and boom! Zafira.

NEIGHBOUR: Zafira? Oh god. Is she okay?

CHLOE: She's hurt bad, but she's mending.

NEIGHBOUR: Oh thank god for that! How are your mum and dad?

CHLOE: Gutted, we're all gutted. Mum and dad more though cos they were only looking after her while Jenny had her hair done.

NEIGHBOUR: Oh they must be gutted!

CHLOE: They are! Hollowed-out they are. You think I look bad, you should see them. Up all night all of us. Jenny's beside herself. I hope she don't blame mum and dad because you know what they're like at that age.

NEIGHBOUR: You can't control them.

CHLOE: You can't control them! They don't know! They don't think! Lord, if she dies...

NEIGHBOUR: Don't even think about it, love, it's not going to happen... Oh little love, have you seen her?

CHLOE: Poor thing. Her hair has been shaved off, stitches everywhere, bandaged up. She peed all over the carpet but you can't say nothing, can you?

NEIGHBOUR: Oh no, love, that's just dogs, isn't it?

CHLOE: Yeah.

Snippets from a Six-Year-Old

i) Nancy has just been asked whether she'd like to join the school choir, which just seconds ago, she'd been rhapsodising about.

NANCY: Oh, Mummy, I don't want to be in the choir!

MUMMY: Why not, darling, I thought you'd enjoy it?

NANCY: But all they ever do is sing!

ii) Nancy has been telling mummy that she's been singing a Christmas carol at school ahead of the Yuletide show.

MUMMY: Oh that's nice, darling. Do you know what's it's called?

NANCY: (withering) No, Mummy, it's in Gerrrrr-man.

iii) Nancy very crossly relates her day.

NANCY: Today we had visitors and they talked about God and Jesus in the Laborious Kingdom. (sniffs and wrinkles her nose) What's *that* all about?

School's Out

A mature student is describing his sister's recent visit.

STUDENT: I was trying to kill time while we waited for the pizza man to turn up so I took Kate on a quick tour of the flat. Kate's a bit reserved so we're keeping it light and everyone's been asked to quieten it down for the night, you know. Anyway, so we flit around – you know, this is my room, this is Joely's room, this is the lounge, dooh dah, dooh dah. Anyway, we're chatting about something when we walk in the kitchen and BOING! There's my flatmate, Joely, in like six-inch spike heels, fishnets, leather knickers, a completely see-through basque top, full war-paint, a spiky collar and dog's lead 'round her neck, stood by the cooker stirring a pan of baked beans. I knew she went to clubs and stuff but I'd never seen her in the full gear before so all I can think to say quickly is, 'And this is Joely. She's a teacher.' My sister, God bless her, just smiles ever so sweetly and says, 'Oh yes? Primary or secondary?'

Sculptures

Mummy is trying to read the paper while seven-year-old Annabel plays and daddy washes up.

ANNABEL: Mummy? Isn't it true that sculptures eat dead people?

MUMMY: Hmmm?

ANNABEL: (crossly) I *say-ed* isn't it true that sculptures eat dead people!

MUMMY: Hey, Snodgrass!

ANNABEL: *I was asking you a question!*

MUMMY: Well, I'm sorry, darling, I was trying to read. Now, what is it you want to know?

ANNABEL: Do. Sculptures. Eat. Dead. People?

MUMMY: No, we've talked about this, darling. Sculptures are often of dead people. But not all the time.

ANNABEL: No! *You're not listening to me!* It was on television!

Daddy enters.

MUMMY: Darling, do you have any idea what Annabel's on about because Mummy is obviously an idiot?

DADDY: Annabel was watching a wildlife programme this morning. I think you mean *vultures* don't you, darling?

ANNABEL: That's what I *say-ed*!

Burning Bright

At a countryside wildlife park – the façade of which is dominated by images of its pair of captive tigers – a party of kids on a trip approach the tiger enclosure.

As they approach the clearly labelled 'tiger enclosure' visitors are able to see large signs carrying illustrations of each tiger, their names, and a detailed description of the species of tiger to be found captive within the tiger enclosure.

A bored-looking kid approaches the compound and visibly brightens.

KID: Aw, look! Lions!

Not Being Minnie Driver

A well-known actress, slightly the worse for wear, descends on a young woman at a celebrity birthday party.

ACTRESS: Oh you're her, aren't you?

WOMAN: I'm sorry.

ACTRESS: Darling, you're her, you're Minnie Driver!

WOMAN: I'm sorry. You've got the wrong person.

ACTRESS: No, darling, don't tease. You are her, you *know* you are.

WOMAN: Honestly I'm not. Isn't she a brunette?

ACTRESS: Darling, I won't hear another word. You are her, and it's...it's *delightful*.

WOMAN: Listen, I'm sorry and everything, but I'm really not her!

ACTRESS: I'm sorry, darling, but you are.

WOMAN: (sighing) Okay, okay, if it makes you happy, then yes, I am Minnie Driver.

ACTRESS: You see! You see! You are! I told you! I'm never wrong about these things. Never!

Expressing Creativity

Two young mums are pushing buggies through the park.

MUM 1: My husband is useless. I know he loves the kids but it really, really, irritates me that he won't bath them.

MUM 2: Really? Why won't he? Most dads love that bit.

MUM 1: I suppose it goes back to when we had just had Neil and we were terrified of this tiny little baby. Terrified that we were going to hurt him. But they aren't little babies now and every night I have to do it. He comes in from work and I would like him to just take them off my hands for a bit.

MUM 2: I know what you mean.

MUM 1: He's not all bad, but he doesn't control them either. The other evening I went out. When I came back there were clothes everywhere, everything was pulled out of the drawers and left on the floor. I said, 'What on earth's been going on here?' And he said, 'Oh, they've been *expressing their creativity*.' Expressing their creativity, my arse! He's not the one who has to iron it all!

The Alison Technique

A patient is occupying the dentist's chair as the dentist and Alison, the rather sullen young dental nurse, prepare.

DENTIST: Right! Now, what are we here for today...? Ah, just a small filling and a clean. Right, if you can just pop your mouth open we'll take a look. That's it. Now, turn towards me...Oh yes, piece of cake. I won't need to use any anaesthetic here. But if you do start to feel something or you need me to stop, just raise your arm. If it really, really hurts, just punch Alison here. No, no! Only joking! Although I do worry that someone might take me seriously one day... Right, okay. Are we ready?

PATIENT: As I'll ever be.

DENTIST: Ah ha ha ha ha ha ha! Good answer! Right then, I'm just going to start with a little bit of drilling, okay? Now open wide. That's it! Good.

Drilling begins.

DENTIST: (to Alison) I'm thinking of doing some more private work, which means we'll have to come in Saturdays. Are you up for that?

ALISON: Saturdays? No way!

DENTIST: Well, we'll see. It will be time and a half, obviously.

ALISON: Not interested.

184

DENTIST: It's just going to be one Saturday a month.

ALISON: No, no way.

DENTIST: Will you think about it then?

ALISON: No point. I'm not working Saturdays.

DENTIST: Well, will you at least think about thinking about it?

Silence.

DENTIST: Double time?

ALISON: I'll think about thinking about it.

DENTIST: There you go! I knew we could work it out!
(To patient) Okay, now rinse.

The Grass Being Greener

Teachers chew the fat following a departmental meeting.

JEN: Oh lord, I've got six little girls coming round for tea tomorrow.

OTHERS: Eeeek!

LAURA: I didn't find it too bad when I had ten round for Ella's birthday.

JEN: Yes but that was in summer, you've got a garden *and* your house is bigger!

LAURA: Urgh, I know! I know! Ella had one of her friends round for tea the other day and her mum's a single parent. She picked her daughter up and said our playroom was as large as their entire ground floor and I thought, oops, it probably is. All of my friends have *huge* houses. Now we're splitting up I think I'll have to find poorer friends.

DEPARTMENT HEAD: Don't you just hate these wealthy people?

DEPARTMENT TECHNICIAN: Grrr. I have a friend I can only cope with seeing once or twice a year. Her life is just so *perfect* I leave feeling completely inadequate.

DEPARTMENT HEAD: Yeas Well we've got the millionaires coming next week so we'll get to hear about their Swiss chalet and the extension they're having slapped on the mansion.

LAURA: So who is it that's got the money? Her or him?

DEPARTMENT HEAD: Well he's a partner in a law firm so he earns about a billion pounds a week and she's in finance. Although she only works two days a week we reckon she probably earns both of our salaries combined. Twice!

Department head furrows his brow and starts petulantly fiddling with his fingernails and fidgeting.

LAURA: Well, I may be about to lose pretty much everything, but I still think I'm lucky really. I mean, at least we're not dying of cancer and having to leave letters to our children.

Laura suddenly slaps the department head hard on the leg.

DEPARTMENT HEAD: Ow!

LAURA: Pay attention! Stop obsessing about yourself and listen to me!

Mixed Messages

A department store at opening time, the cleaner is still polishing the floor. The ground-floor menswear department is being prepared for the day.

CAMP SALES ASSISTANT: Yeuch, slippery, isn't it? Oh, Lucy, you know what used to get me? Those accident prevention films. Do you remember them? They used to be on TV all the time when I was little. Before everything shut down or in a morning in the kids programmes. Remember? They usually had old people in them, and you knew something was going to happen, like granny was going to trip on the rug and smash her head open. My favourite was, 'Don't stand on high things,' and oh, there was Granddad in his stripy flannel pyjamas and his tartan slippers, falling on his arse. Oh, Lucy, I did laugh! I laughed until I cried!

Milk with Three

A brickie is travelling through south west London by commuter train. He makes a mobile phone call.

BRICKIE: Don't you "allo me, Jaffa! Wot?' I've just bin to collect me tools ain't I? Nah, wen' out wiv Vinnie didn' I? Left 'em in the luggage rack. Vinnie? Nah, he was in the baggage car when I left 'im. Dunno, mate. Hastings I suppose. Yeah, I'll be ten facking minutes, all right? Wot? Nah, mate, he's gotta pay. Nah, the kid was 'ere all facking day, he's gotta be paid. Nah, the geezers gotta pay day-work for that. Nah, I'll tell 'im meself. 'E was 'ere all facking day waiting for the facking scaffolder to turn up. Nah, it was still going up at five when I left. He did some canting around but nothing you could 'ang it on, if you know wot I mean. Nah, fella's gotta pay, and he's gotta pay the gargoyle an' all! Yeah. Nah, nah, ten minutes my son. Yeah, milk with three, ta. Yeah, you an' all. Sweet.

Bladdy Tourists!

An Englishman makes an innocent enquiry in New South Wales.

TOURIST: Have you got anything with a map of the area on it?

TOURIST INFORMATION OFFICER 1: What, you mean like an area map?

TOURIST INFORMATION OFFICER 2: Yeah, our area maps have got maps on them.

TOURIST: That sounds exactly like the kind of thing I'm looking for. Thank you.

Silence.

TOURIST INFORMATION OFFICER 1: So would you like a map then?

Jeffrey & the Tramp

A lefty media-type is recounting a tale over cocktails and salted cashews.

RYAN: So I was living up north then and every weekend I'd drive back down to my parents in Cambridge for a little rest and recuperation from the job. Anyway, I'd just got the MG and because it was summer I was driving with the top down. It was the real deal, do you know what I mean? Every now and then I'd get a little left-wing pang of conscience about polluting the environment in this highly desirable, bourgeois sports car.

DAN: But not often?

RYAN: But not often. Anyway, on this particular Saturday I'm driving along when I see this old guy thumbing for a lift beside the road. He doesn't look too smart, and I'm just thinking he looks like a tramp when this pang of conscience jabs me...

DAN: Ah, the liberal lefty pang.

RYAN: Well exactly. So I roll to a stop and ask him where he's going. 'Cambridge,' he says, so I think, oh well, fair enough and tell him to hop in. Well of course he's hidden this enormous great sleeping bag and all his belongings behind the nearest bush so as not to put a potential lift off. So now I have to help him secure this frankly rank package to the back of the MG. Anyway, it's all done and we set off. Lucky it is an open top-type of day because my passenger clearly hasn't seen a bathtub for a year or two. So for the next twenty or so miles there's very little conversation from me because I don't want to open my mouth and taste the stench.

DAN: In a caring liberal lefty way.

RYAN: Now, as we start approaching Cambridge I ask him where exactly he's going, to which he replies, 'Oh just take me where you're going.' And I'm thinking, oh no, matey! This is where my charitable spirit peters out. I don't mind giving you a lift and having to have the car steam-cleaned, but you're not coming to my parent's house. So I politely but firmly suggest that maybe I should drop him in the middle of town. Well, he's not happy about that.

DAN: He clearly has standards.

RYAN: Absolutely. Apparently he gets more in the way of handouts from smaller communities, but if I happened to know where there was a vicarage, then to drop him there because vicarages are a good place to get food and a handout. Well, like most people, I suppose I don't know that many vicars. Then it occurred to me that while I didn't know many vicars there was a very expensive former vicarage nearby that might suit both his and my purposes. It just so happens that it belonged to two of my very favourite people, Jeffrey and Mary Archer.

DAN: You didn't!

RYAN: I did. I dropped my passenger off at the end of the drive, pointed him in the direction of the front door and skiddaddled before anyone could stop me. God, I hope Jeffrey was the one who opened the door!

Jessica's News

A mother relates her daughter's earlier sins to her intended.

MOTHER: Oh she was a little bugger for only giving you one side of the story. One day I went into school for parents' evening and the teacher seems to be asking me all sorts of funny questions about life at home. Eventually she just starts laughing and says to me, 'I'm sorry, but I've got to show you this.' So she brings out this piece that Jessica has written, 'My news.' Apparently they wrote it every Monday so that the teachers got some idea of what they got up to over the weekend. So I quickly read it, and basically it says, 'On Saturday we went to three pubs and Martin and I had two Coca Colas and a packet of crisps. When we got home in the afternoon mummy got up. On Sunday we only went to one pub and I helped Daddy clean out the bottles from behind the sofa.' Well, you can imagine what that must have sounded like! What she hadn't told them was that her dad was illustrating a pub guide, and mummy was a night nurse and the bottles were there because her Dad was home-brewing at the time. Honestly, they must have been ready to send in the social services!

Royal Insecurity

A barman discusses his previous employment.

BARMAN: I kid you not, when you were hired to work as a waiter or ice cream hander-outer at one of the Queen's garden parties you were given a questionnaire to fill in with questions like 'Do you want to kill the Royal Family?' or 'Are you a member of any known terrorist organisation?' MI5 are really on the ball, aren't they?

The Lost Aisle

One of Britain's most respected celebrity travel writers/TV presenters is pulling a battered old suitcase through a newsagents at Kings Cross Station. He is guided towards Time *magazine by a male shop assistant who hasn't recognised him.*

ASSISTANT: That's it, straight down that aisle, left, no, left, left. That's right. No that's the wrong effing way! Never mind, carry on straight now. Now right, that's it, that's it, now right. Right again, straight on... Now left. Can you see it? Next to the financial magazines. No, that's the puzzles... Oh I give up.

Storms down the aisle to lend assistance.

ASSISTANT: (Under his breath) Gawd help anyone who ever gets directions off you, you old duffer.

Stripping Off

Weary parents are discussing decorating at the school gate.

GARY: Nah, I do it all. I don't *like* it, but I do it.

FRAN: Wot I 'ate is 'e starts a job and 'e thinks 'e's got enough paint and everythin' an' then 'e starts and it's, 'oh no I ain't got enuff.' Then it's 'Oh right, now we've gotta wait till 'e can get down to 'omebase again.'

GARY: And if you ain't got the car or you don't drive...

ANDREA: Oh I do all the decorating in my 'ouse. 'E can't do it. 'opeless 'e is. Tell ya, he tried to put up wallpaper once. I said, you don't wanna try that, 'e says 'Sling yer hook.' So anyway, he thinks, I won't bovver stripping off the wallpaper that's on, I'll just go over it. Anyway, I gets 'ome from work and 'e's stood in the livin room wiv all this wallpaper curled on the floor.

GARY: Oh no!

ANDREA: I'm telling ya, 'e is *not* impressed! Ooh I did larf!

So, Do You Know Liam?

On a train out of Victoria a Mancunian in his early twenties is talking to two teenage girls, Tray and Kaz.

TRAY: So do you know Liam, then?

MANCUNIAN: Ah, Liam, he's a boy he is. I know his brother better though...

KAZ: So what's biggest gig you've played?

MANCUNIAN: T in the Park. Noel came on with us for a song at that.

KAZ: You know him a lot then?

MANCUNIAN: Yeah, he's our manager like.

TRAY: You've got it made then, ain't ya?

MANCUNIAN: Ah, I don't know about that. Our singer used to go to school with him like so he's helping us out. To be honest, he's a bit frustrating sometimes. You see, he's already done everything like, and cos we haven't and we're new to it like, he'll say to us, 'you don't wanna be doing that', and we're like, 'c'mon, man, we just wanna like try, you know?

KAZ: Yeah. So does he always play with you like?

MANCUNIAN: Nah, just occasionally. Next year we'll be doing all festivals, you know?

TRAY: I don't like festivals.

KAZ: Yeah, you get wet.

MANCUNIAN: We were in Finland yesterday! You should check us out in autumn, girls. We're supporting Oasis at Shepherds Bush. Come on down and check us out. We've got an album out an all.

KAZ: Is it good?

MANCUNIAN: Yeah, it's the nuts. But then I would say that, wouldn't I?

KAZ: Yeah.

TRAY: Yeah.

MANCUNIAN: (getting up at Battersea park) Anyway, girls, this is my stop. Remember though, Shepherds Bush Empire. Come down and check us out, yeah?

KAZ: Yeah, all right.

MANCUNIAN: (getting off the train) I'll be looking out for youse.

TRAY: Tar-ra! (pause) Who was he?

KAZ: Dunno. Phil something? He's the drummer anyway.

TRAY: And what were the band called?

KAZ: Dunno. Did he keep winking at you?

TRAY: Yeah.

KAZ: Ugh!

TRAY: Yeah, ugh

Ageing Michelle

Ruth and Louise, two mature ladies, chat on a park bench in the early spring sunshine, while Ruth's husband, Frank, peruses the sports pages.

LOUISE: Oooh, fancy!

RUTH: I know!

LOUISE: How old was she?

RUTH: She's not young. Well, she's not *young*, young. She was Michelle's age. Wasn't she, Frank? Wasn't she Michelle's age? She was Michelle's age. No... hang on... No, she was born in December, which makes her... She was! She was, wasn't she? She was Michelle's age! Wasn't she? Frank? Wasn't she, Frank?

FRANK: Who's Michelle?

Fashionable

Grandpa, on hearing that his grandson has been diagnosed as being on the autistic spectrum.

GRANDPA: Humph. At least he's got something fashionable.

Culture

A staffroom cynic responds to the government's initiative to introduce school children to five hours' worth of culture a week.

CYNIC: Culture, my arse! How's that going to fit in with everything else we're supposed to be doing for them then? And anyway, how many bloody MPs do you think experience five hours of culture every week, hmm? Culture, my *arse*! You try taking a group of year nines to the opera!

RSVP

Two women drink coffee and weak tea in a cafe in Yorkshire.

1: I have to say I'm very, *very* grateful to you for the invitation...

2: Not at all...

1: But I should make it very clear that if I didn't know you, that is if I only knew you as a person at work rather than as a real person, then I wouldn't come.

2: Oh.

1: You see, if I came along without knowing you, I wouldn't know anyone there, would I? Now what's the point of being somewhere where you don't know anybody, eh?

2: Yes, I can see that...

1: I mean, I might not have anything in common with these people, and I don't like to think that I'm somewhere where I don't have anything in common with people. Especially strangers.

2: No, that makes sense...

1: I mean, put me down as a definite 'yes', but I'll make my mind up on the morning, if that's okay with you?

2: That's, erm, perfectly fine.

1: I mean, last year at your barbecue, I hardly knew you, and I didn't know any other bugger there and do you know what?

2: No?

1: I felt stupid, that's what. I didn't know anyone, so I didn't talk to anyone, I don't drink and I don't eat barbecued food so as I'm sure you'll understand, I just felt really stupid being there.

2: You enjoyed yourself though.

1: Oh yes, I enjoyed myself, but it didn't stop me feeling stupid. Now, if I do come, what sort of present should I bring him?

2: Oh I don't know. What are two year olds into these days?

Santi

A Dad is in the local play park with his kids when someone else's four-year-old son jumps on his foot.

DAD: Ouch, that erm...

OTHER DAD: Santi! What on earth are you doing? You apologise to that man immediately!

Santi digs a little hole in the sandpit with one foot while staring up at the man, a half-smile on his lips and a little glimmer in his eyes.

SANTI: Sorry, *man.*

Taking Direction from Stanley Kubrick

Nicola on hearing of the death of the director Stanley Kubrick.

NICOLA: I was quite friendly with Stanley Kubrick's daughter when we were at school. They lived quite close and I'd go over and play there sometimes. My mother delights in telling everyone that I came home one day and she asked me if I'd had a nice time and I said yes, but I thought that their house had a very odd name. Oh yes? she said. And what's it called? To which I innocently replied, Tradesmen's Entrance.

The Bottom Line

Mums sneaking a cabernet sauvignon 'fruit juice' in the garden.

ALLIE: I just love the way children know the exact moment to bring something up and embarrass you. The other morning the phone rang and I rushed to answer it from the loo. It was my boss and just as I was answering it, Lizzy shouts out at full volume, 'It's rude not to pull your knickers up!'

MEL: Oh that's a good one! But they are just fascinated by bottoms and rudeness. My little one managed to shout out in the swimming pool changing rooms that mummy had a willy.

ANGELA: Oh yes, Sam, is always scrutinising me and asking me why I haven't got a willy. I suppose it must seem strange for him because his dad and brother do. It's funny, I don't mind walking around the house naked and letting the children see me. But, I don't know about you, but it does feel wrong to talk to my dad on the phone when I'm not wearing anything.

MEL: Oh god, yeah! And kids have that knack of asking embarrassing questions at the wrong time.

ALLIE: I did really well the other morning. Lizzy asked why her bottom had two holes. I'd been waiting for that one! I did well though because Marcus copped for it. It was Saturday morning and he was letting me have a lie-in. I got up at nine and found he had dealt with that difficult little question *and* managed to get the border up in the spare room.

The Muralist's Tales

An artist is painting a mural at a south London train station. A man with a very high-pitched voice appears at the artist's shoulder.

MAN: What's this, then?

ARTIST: It's to help brighten up the station. A group of local kids came up with the design and I'm painting it for them.

MAN: Oh. I like digging holes! Yes, I like digging holes! Down by the Thames. I find all sorts of things. Last Sunday I found a monk's cup. Down by the Thames, would you believe? Don't know how old it is, I'll take it to the V&A. Last year I found a medal. See, I'm a bit of a spiritualist and I think that I was a monk in a former life. Mmmmn. Yes, I like colours and I like sculpture. Yes. Nice talking to you. Bye.

Later, a mum and her daughter pause to look at the mural.

GIRL: Look, Mum, it's changed! Look, the spaceman's hands have changed! They used to go this way and now they go that way. The children did it!

MOTHER: What? Has it been vandalised already? Oh, what a shame.

GIRL: The children did it!

MOTHER: That's terrible, and it's not even finished. Still, it's just asking for it really, isn't it? Doing something like this in a public place.

ARTIST: It hasn't been vandalised, the children that designed it asked for some changes to be made.

MOTHER: Oh. Awful shame though, isn't it? I don't know why you bother.

LATER STILL. An elderly man in a flat cap pauses by the mural and sneers critically.

MAN: I suppose you've been to art school then! My daughter's an artist. St Martin's. Not the way I'd want to earn a living, it scares the pants off me. She painted some columns on the Docklands Railway... How long will this take you?

ARTIST: Four weeks. I can only work a short day because they won't allow me to be here during rush hour.

MAN: Did you win a competition?

ARTIST: No, there's a group of local youngsters who belong to an environmental forum. They put forward the idea as a way to brighten up the station and came up with the design. It shows travel in the past, present and future.

MAN: (long pause) Yes, well, you see my daughter won a competition to do the pillars. A national competition. Mind you, it was all abstract. Could have been anything. Well, must go. I'm visiting my brother in hospital. Anyway, good luck to you. Not the way I'd want to earn a living. Scares the pants off me.

The Phantom Pregnancy

An expectant father is in a south London pub and in the wrong...
again.

FATHER: Honestly, I can't do anything right lately.

MATE: That's fatherhood, matey, get used to it. What did you
do this time?

FATHER: Twenty-two week scan at the hospital. Car's in the
shop so we're bussing it. I broke my watch Monday so I'm
using the clock on my phone. That's wrong, isn't it? So we're
running for the bus. Get to the pedestrian crossing and the bus
is already at the stop. Fuck. So I sprint across and get there just
as the miserable bleeder is closing his doors. Wife's behind me
like, doing the best she can, and out the corner of my eye I see
this other woman waddling towards the bus. So I pound on the
door but the driver's 'aving none of it. So now I'm pissed off
and I'm shouting, Oi! These two women are expecting! What
do you want them to do? Walk to 'ospital?' So the other
woman's at the door by now and she's got the right 'ump.
'I'm *not* pregnant!' she says! Ooops! Open mouth, insert boot.
Quick as a flash I say, I know, love, I know. But *he* doesn't.

MATE: Get away with it?

FATHER: Nah. And we missed the fucking bus. Longest
fucking twenty minutes of my life waiting for the next bus
that was.

Two Very Different Travellers

A restaurant in central London. An elderly husband engages the head waiter in conversation as he waits for his wife to come back from the loo.

HUSBAND: Now, if I'm not very much mistaken that's an Antipodean accent that you've got there, isn't it? Where are you from, Australia or New Zealand?

HEAD WAITER: Well actually, it's a little more complicated than that, sir. I'm actually Belgian.

HUSBAND: Belgian? Good lord!

HEAD WAITER: But my family emigrated to Australia when I was five so I guess I'm now an Australian.

HUSBAND: My word, so you're bi, are you?

HEAD WAITER: 'scuse me?

HUSBAND: Bi...lingual?

HEAD WAITER: Oh sure! Sorry, I thought you... Yeah, I'm a little rusty on the old French though.

HUSBAND: Oh, you speak French too!

HEAD WAITER: Er yeah, as it happens.

HUSBAND: So what on earth made you give up Australia for miserable rainy old Britain? Don't you miss the sun?

HEAD WAITER: Aw, you know. Anyway, Australia isn't such a sweet place to be any more.

HUSBAND: No? Good lord. It always looks rather pleasant on TV.

HEAD WAITER: Yeah, well, where my folks live they've had a drought for ten years.

HUSBAND: Ten years?! Good lord!

HEAD WAITER: Nothing will grow, all the water is gone, the animals are dying and the aborigines are being forced into the city. I'm telling you, it's just a bloody dustbowl.

The wife returns.

HUSBAND: Extraordinary. Ten years...

HEAD WAITER: And it's the rest of the world to blame. Countries like this and America in particular. China! Japan! Global warming. They reckon in fifty years Australia will be uninhabitable, and we're just sitting back and letting it happen. Aw, I tell you...

Head waiter exits to take an order.

WIFE: That sounded very intense.

HUSBAND: Yes. Rum bugger. I only asked him where he was from.

Mental Lentils

A lady of impeccable character comes clean.

JESSICA: The shopping had just been delivered and I'd been busy packing things away. As I was busy sis insisted on rustling up some lunch so she put these lentils on to go with something or other. Anyway, we're just about to serve them up when I noticed that there were all these little black bits in them. They turn out to be little flies and when we look in the packet it's crawling with them and now so is the cupboard they came from. So sis throws a complete paddy and insists that I phone the supermarket and tell them what has happened. The manager sounds absolutely distraught and promptly turns up on our doorstep about twenty minutes later with a full week's worth of shopping as compensation and a lovely little man with lots of cleaning equipment. While the manager is unpacking all the shopping, the lovely little man is cleaning out all our kitchen cupboards, disinfecting absolutely everything and everywhere. By the time the shopping goes away everything is absolutely spotless. The manager apologises profusely for the inconvenience, promises he will investigate, and begs us not to think badly of the store. After all that, how could you? It was only about ten minutes after he'd gone that I suddenly realised we hadn't actually bought the lentils from *that* supermarket. Alex had bought them at a different store a couple of months ago. Oh I felt awful!

In a Hole

A café in Bedfordshire on a Sunday afternoon. A man is chatting on his mobile while his girlfriend sullenly stirs her cappuccino to death.

MAN: Nah. Clutch. Nah, that's wot 'e said it woz...Well I dunno, I ain't a bladdy mechanic! It's five years old...Eh? You what? Really? What? In 'ole? Innan 'ole? Really? Fack! In an 'ole! Wot, on the telly? Nah? It's on the telly? Re-sult! Gotta tell Di. Nah, gotta tell Di. Innan 'ole, eh? Cor! Yeah laters, mate.

He ends the call.

MAN: You'll never guess wot.

GIRLFRIEND: Wot?

MAN: Go on! Guess!

GIRLFRIEND: Wot?

MAN: All right, all right keep yer 'air on! They've only gonnan fahnd Saddam ain't they?

GIRLFRIEND: Yeah?

MAN: Yeah! Innan 'ole.

GIRLFRIEND: Innan 'ole?

MAN: Yeah, straight up. Innan 'ole. 'Son the telly.

GIRLFRIEND: Coo.

MAN: Too right! 'ere, I've gotta tell Danny.

Punches a key on his phone.

MAN: Danny boy? Tel. 'Ere they've only gonnan fahnd 'im. Saddam! Yeah, yeah. Innan 'ole, mate. In a fackin' 'ole.

Fruit

A former hotel worker besmirches the image of a Hollywood legend.

HOTEL WORKER: Oh yeah, lovely guy. If an apple or orange in one of the complimentary fruit baskets was even just a fraction past its best he would stab it repeatedly with a letter opener and make us take it to the manager.

Expectations

A little boy has been agitating to visit the gift shop at a visitor attraction – a combined garden and mill. Finally his grandma gets the message.

GRANDMA: Oh of course we can, love! I bet we can find something you'll like... Now, let's see... Ooh I know! How about a little bag of flour?

Everybody Loves Madeira

On a commuter train into London two mature ladies discuss an acquaintance's recent holiday.

SARAH: Where'd they go?

FRANCES: I don't know exactly. Somewhere on the Red Sea.

SARAH: Madeira?

FRANCES: No, love, Madeira isn't on the Red Sea.

SARAH: Oh you're right, sorry! Silly old moo. It was Manilla, wasn't it?

FRANCES: Something like that.

SARAH: Didn't they have trouble?

FRANCES: No! Well, the plane did land on one engine, but no, they had a lovely time. But they were going to Petra so...

SARAH: Ah!

FRANCES: Yes!

SARAH: It's so hot though, isn't it?

FRANCES: It is! They said the security in the airport was very good though.

SARAH: She suffers really badly from jet lag.

FRANCES: Does she?

SARAH: Oh yes! She keeps her bed made up ready!

FRANCES: Is it a timeshare?

SARAH: Well I don't know if it's a timeshare, but they do share it with somebody part-time... Everybody loves Madeira though, don't they?

FRANCES: They do! It's very hilly though.

SARAH: Yes.

Ten Seconds of Fame

A middle-aged wit and raconteur is holding court amongst a pub crowd of young meeja types.

WIT: I *am* a star of the silver screen. I'll have you know I give the definitive performance as 'man sitting on a bar stool drinking white wine' in a Radiohead video.

CATHY: Oh wow that *is* cred.

WIT: Yes I thought so. Although when I gathered friends together for a public screening of my crowning triumph my actual screen debut was missed as we chose that exact moment in the film to hunt for a bottle opener that I'd just dropped.

CATHY: Were you on screen long?

WIT: Not really. If Andy Warhol was right I suspect that I still have roughly fourteen minutes and fifty seconds of fame still to be allocated to me. However I'm confident the phone call from Cannes is imminent. God I hope us boring old fortysomethings haven't been boring the pants off you young teenager types with our tales of past glories?

CATHY: No. It's nice. It reminds me of my Dad.

WIT: Right, and with that little bombshell, I think I should probably drink up and go don't you?

Rabbit

Teacher B walks into the classroom to chat to Teacher A. On the way in he spots Beth, one of his former pupils.

TEACHER B: Hello, Beth, how are you?

BETH: I've got a rabbit!

TEACHER B: I er, oh, right. Why?

BETH: It was a Valentine's present!

TEACHER B: Riiiight...

TEACHER A: And did you want a rabbit?

BETH: Well we talked about animals ages ago, and I said I liked rabbits so Kieran said he was going to buy me one. I chose it myself from the pet shop!

TEACHER A: Okay, so what's it called?

BETH: Rosie! It's a house rabbit! My mum wasn't very pleased...

TEACHER A: Yes, I can imagine...

BETH: She came home in such a good mood! Then she saw we'd already set up the cage.

TEACHER B: Rosie the rabbit... You know, Beth, I don't have conversations like this at my home.

BETH: Well that's good cos that way you know when you're at work, don't you!

The Rastafarian Good Food Guide

An elderly Rastafarian man comes crashing through the connecting doors of a north bound underground train. He does a double take when he sees two WPCs and strides up to them laughing. Both women's posture changes. They rest their hands on their batons.

WPC 1: Aye, aye...

RASTA: (still laughing) Lookit you! In all this. Many shiny tings. Ha ha haaa. And lookit you! All sorry. Ha ha haaa.

WPC 1: Having a good evening, sir?

RASTA: (shouting) What? What? I'm so hungry now!

WPC 2: Shhhhh. Now, now, no need to shout, we can hear you. Where are you off to, sir?

RASTA: Aaaaah Peckham!

WPC 2: Peckham?

WPC 1: Not on this train you're not, sir.

RASTA: I go anywhere I want!

WPC 2: But this train isn't going to Peckham, sir?

WPC 1: You're not even going in the right direction.

RASTA: Balham then!

WPC 1: It's not going there either.

RASTA: Finsbury Park!

WPC 2: Okay, but you'll have to change at Warren Street.

RASTA: Where you going? You got ticket?

WPC 1: We don't need tickets, sir, we're on duty.

RASTA: (shouting) Betcha going to the station. Betcha going to your canteen! Betcha got all good things to eat in your canteen!

WPC 2: Ssshhh.

RASTA: Sshhhh now. Betcha got eggs... and ham... and sausages... and shepherd's pie...

WPC 1: Oh god...

RASTA: ...and beetroot... and pickle... and fishcakes... and broccoli... and rice crispies...

The train halts and the two WPCs exit. The Rastafarian man follows them off the train.

RASTA: ...and pomegranates... and pasta... and sweet potato... and chips... and jam... and baked beans... and brussel sprouts... and teacakes...

His voice can be heard echoing down the tunnel until the train doors eventually close.

Charity

A train travels through the Midlands towards London. A young woman is slaving away on a laptop and notepad. At a small station a man gets on and rustles into the seat opposite her.

MAN: Eh, I don't know, you'll have all your work done before you get to London!

WOMAN: Oh I wish!

MAN: Lots to do?

WOMAN: Oh yes.

Silence.

MAN: Where *you* travelling from?

WOMAN: Leicester.

MAN: Leicester? Ooh, they've got a right nice Sainsbury's there, haven't they?

WOMAN: Um yes, I suppose it is quite a nice one.

MAN: Oh it's *right* nice that one. And *big*!

Silence.

MAN: We've Tescos.

Silence. The woman nods kindly then tries to bury her nose in her work. Other travellers have begun to exchange looks and wince on the young woman's behalf. Then...

MAN: I'm going to Luton.

WOMAN: Hmm?

MAN: I'm going to Luton. Shopping.

WOMAN: Oh... Nice.

MAN: I'll probably have a few drinks but I don't think I'll get hammered today.

WOMAN: Mmmm.

MAN: Just four or five maybe... I like that Magners you know!

WOMAN: Riiight.

Silence.

MAN: Do you like Magners?

WOMAN: You know I don't think I've ever tried it.

MAN: It's right nice cold. I like a drink when we're playing games. You know, Scrabble, Draughts, Snakes & Ladders, chess... Do you like Scrabble?

WOMAN: Mmm!

Silence.

MAN: I work in a kitchen. It's *very* stressful.

WOMAN: Hm?

MAN: I only wash up, I don't cook.

WOMAN: Mmm.

MAN: It's not so busy now. August were busy. It weren't as busy as normal though.

WOMAN: O-kay...

MAN: Been a bit indifferent this year.

WOMAN: Riiight. That because of the weather?

MAN: Dunno.

WOMAN: Riiiiiight.

Silence.

MAN: I like shopping. CDs, bacon... Do you like bacon?

WOMAN: Mmmm...

MAN: Beans... And *mushrooms*! Eh, mushrooms go down nice, don't they?

WOMAN: Um...

MAN: We have roast on Mondays. Course it's only me and me Dad now Mum's gone... Beef, pork, lamb... Big fan of lamb I am.

WOMAN: Uh-huh.

Silence.

MAN: What's *your* favourite meat?

And thus it continued all the way to Luton...

Get a Job

A teacher is encouraging a student to apply himself.

TEACHER: You know, if you really focused your energy on this project you could get it done in a week.

WILL: I know, miss, it's just that I've been waiting to hear if I've got a job, and if I haven't, that means I've got to look for one and once I've got one then I'll know when I'm working and when I'm not. D'you know what I mean?

TEACHER: I thought you already had a job?

WILL: Yeah, Debenhams, but it was temporay. There're jobs with Woolworths but I don't want to work at Woolworths. The people are nice but I just don't like Woolworths.

TEACHER: Is Marks & Spencer more your line then?

WILL: Oh no! No, I couldn't work with food. Well I *could*. I mean, I'm very hygienic, but I might get all obsessive compulsive or something. You know, always washing my hands and stuff.

TEACHER: You could work in menswear.

WILL: I'd be just as bad in there! I'd have to have all the hangers the right way and the sizes in the right order. Oh no, couldn't do that... I'm all right with homewares!

Headucation

A bemused young mum emerges from a primary school meeting on their use of synthetic phonics.

MUM: But I thought artificial things were supposed to be bad for them!

I Wanna be Adopted

A mum and her little girl are having a picnic in the park.

DAUGHTER: Mummy, what's adopted mean?

MUM: It's when a child can't live with its real parents because they've died or something.

DAUGHTER: Why did they die?

MUM: I don't know! But then other adults come along and offer to look after the child, love it and raise it as their own.

DAUGHTER: But why did the parents have to die? Did someone kill them?

MUM: Noooo. Look, I *don't know* why they died! Maybe they didn't! But the important thing is that someone comes along and takes care of the child!

The daughter cogitates on this for a while.

DAUGHTER: Mummy?

MUM: Yeeee-es?

DAUGHTER: Am I adopted?

Management Material

A grandmother is reminiscing to her teenage granddaughter.

GRANDMOTHER: Your Dad and his brothers were horrors when they were your age. Then your Dad and Lynn were living together with Peter, a friend of theirs. Lynn was just about to start training as a store manager, so he thought he'd better have some fun before he forgot how. Anyway, it was very fashionable for young men to wear bowler hats back then, and Peter was very proud of his. So your Dad bought two bowler hats, one a size too small, one a size too big, and they'd swap them around every other day so poor Peter didn't know what the hell was going on. I think he thought he'd caught a disease, bless 'im.

All Change

A smartly dressed woman is walking past a cubicle in the changing rooms of a high street fashion store when the curtain flies back and a half-dressed woman brandishes a jumper at her.

HALF-DRESSED WOMAN: Can you get me this in the next size up, please?

SMARTLY DRESSED WOMAN: I don't work here.

HALF-DRESSED WOMAN: (tutting) Oh well, you look like someone who should.

She slides the curtain back.

SMARTLY DRESSED WOMAN: I'm not quite sure how to take that.

Blackies

A couple have brought an elderly and hard of hearing relative out to enjoy the scenery around Ladybower Reservoir in Derbyshire. The couple are buying ice creams when a new Mercedes pulls into the parking area. Out of the car steps a young black family. The wife has a sleepy baby in her arms.

ELDERLY RELATIVE: (loudly) Eeee, look at them. Blackies wi' that car!

GRANDDAUGHTER: Grandma!

ELDERLY RELATIVE: (loudly) Eee, you wouldn't have thought blackies could afford a car like that, would you?

GRANDDAUGHTER: Grandma, please! Shush!

ELDERLY RELATIVE: (loudly) What's the matter, love? Hey up I'm losing me cone here!

HUSBAND: It's grand here, innit? Lovely green fields, all that granite on t'hills and sun ont' watter eh, love?

ELDERLY RELATIVE: (loudly) Oh aye, it's lovely. I'm reet grateful tha' you brought me.

GRANDDAUGHTER: It's lovely for us to have you with us, Grandma.

ELDERLY RELATIVE: (loudly) Eee, you could just drink it in, couldn't you?

GRANDDAUGHTER: Aye.

HUSBAND: Aye.

Pause.

ELDERLY RELATIVE: (loudly) Eeee, look at them. Blackies is buying ice creams!

GRANDDAUGHTER: Grandma!

BLACK MOTHER: (laughing) It's all right love. Don't worry yourself. You 'aving a nice time, love?

ELDERLY RELATIVE: (loudly) Eee, look at that little baby! Isn't he gorgeous!

BLACK MOTHER: Thank you!

ELDERLY RELATIVE: (loudly) Can I 'ave a look?

BLACK MOTHER: Course you can, love!

ELDERLY RELATIVE: (loudly) 'Es grand isn't e? 'E's like a little black monkey...

GRANDDAUGHTER AND HUSBAND: *Grandma!*

A Missed Opportunity

*Two woman chat over the rails in a well-known children's
clothing store.*

WOMAN 1: I said, 'Why don't you come in?' He says, 'I don't
want to.' 'But it's your child being born,' I said. 'You don't
want to miss that!' He says, 'Trust me, I do...' But I think he'll
regret it.

WOMAN 2: Oh he will!

WOMAN 1: He *will*! He'll regret it for the rest of his life.

The Gen on Jenna

A young couple are travelling on a bus in Rotherhem. The girl is scrolling through text messages on her mobile phone when she guffaws.

GIRL: Aw, Jenna! Aw, she's proper funny! Listen what she texted me last night, 'I'm out wi' Ben. Fart. Eaten sommat bad. Fart. Looks like sex is out of the question. Fart.'

The Pottery Shop part 1

It is just before Christmas. A mother and father have taken their daughter to a pottery painting shop and are greeted at the door by one of the proprietors, a middle-aged lady dressed in a comfy country style. The shop is otherwise empty.

SANDRA: Hello! Hello! I'm Sandra! Charlotte's just popped out. Making the most of the, er, *quiet moments*. I'll go later. Er, have you painted pottery before?

The door pings open and Charlotte, a trendily dressed lady of middle years, enters.

SANDRA: Oh *here's* Charlotte. Are you all right, dear? How was it?

CHARLOTTE: It's *murder* out there! People have just gone crazy! You should have seen the queue in Primark...!

She fans herself at the memory.

CHARLOTTE: I went there first because I wanted to get Annabel's pyjamas. I couldn't decide between monkeys or frogs so I saw a girl about her age and asked which she would choose, monkeys or frogs, and she says frogs. So I thought right then, frogs it is! But the *queue*! I mean, they had all the tills open and everyone's working flat out, but oh dear... Anyway, after that, I went to the er... Oh, what's it called? The nut shop?

SANDRA: Oh, where they sell nuts? Do sit down! Anywhere you like!

Mother and daughter seat themselves and father says his goodbyes.

CHARLOTTE: Yes, you know where I mean. So I got a few bags, just a few bits, you know. And I got some more coffee!

SANDRA: Oh good! Shall I put some on?

CHARLOTTE: Ooh yes, why not!

SANDRA: Should I wash the thingy out?

CHARLOTTE: Nooooo, it'll be fine.

SANDRA: That's *just* the answer I wanted! Now, you know this won't be ready for Christmas, don't you?

MOTHER: Oh that's fine. No hurry.

SANDRA: We get a lot of groups just after Christmas, you know. Teachers. Very popular with teachers.

The father has said his goodbyes and his hand is on the door handle when...

SANDRA: Oh, Are you not staying to enjoy the experience?

FATHER: Er, no.

SANDRA: Right, well, your loss.

The Pottery Shop part 2

Mother and daughter are deeply immersed in painting their pottery while Sandra and Charlotte stand nearby drinking coffee.

SANDRA: I saw Jock this morning.

CHARLOTTE: What *Jock*, Jock?

SANDRA: No, the other one. The one with the Mercedes Sport. He is called Jock, isn't he?

CHARLOTTE: Mmmmm...

SANDRA: Anyway, he called out hello as he went under the police tape... He had his white shirt on! All undone, with his chest exposed!

CHARLOTTE: Oooh! It's funny... you know where he lives, don't you?

SANDRA: Er, no. Where?

CHARLOTTE: Up West Hill way.

SANDRA: Oh.

CHARLOTTE: So, you know, nothing *fancy*.

SANDRA: Nooooo. Doesn't really match up with the car and everything, does it?

CHARLOTTE AND SANDRA: Hmmmmmmmm.

Social Skills

Two teenage girls are chatting as they wait for the train from
Queens Park to arrive at Euston.

SOPHIE: I'm telling you, man, it was like well wicked.

ANTHEA: Yeah?

SOPHIE: Yeah, totally!

ANTHEA: How d'you get 'ome?

SOPHIE: That's funny that is.

ANTHEA: Wha'?

SOPHIE: You know Michael?

ANTHEA: Yeah?

SOPHIE: Me and 'im is chillin', innit. And I'm larfing? And
this policewoman comes up and says ''Ere, bit late for that
kind of row, innit?' And I says, 'So?' And she says, 'You wanna
keep it down, love?' And I says, 'I ain't your love.'

ANTHEA: Aw, that's so cool! Wha, she say?

SOPHIE: She says, 'Right, love, no need to be attitudey.' I says,
'Attitudey? What's attitudey?' And she says, 'You giving me
attitude.'

ANTHEA: Aw. What you say?

SOPHIE: Aw, man, I'm all pumped up? I says, 'I ain't being no attitudey.' I says, ''ere, when you was learning to become police, yeah?' She says, 'Yeah.' I says, 'Didn' they learn you how to talk proper?

ANTHEA: You didn'!

SOPHIE: I did!

ANTHEA: Aw no, man!

SOPHIE: I did!

ANTHEA: Wha' she do?

SOPHIE: 'Rested me.

ANTHEA: No!

SOPHIE: Yeah. Thing is, she 'rested me before. Funny, innit? I didn't recognise her.

The Art Lover

Art dealers at an exhibition opening diss a fairweather celebrity client.

ART DEALER: Of course she's a serious art collector. Didn't you see her leaning against the Paula Rego?

Coitus Infinitum

Overheard through a thin wall in a Sheffield flatshare.

MAN: Oh yees! Yeeees! Yes! Yes! Yes! Oh, oh, oh God! Yes. Yeeees! Oh. My God! Yeeeeeeeeeessss! Mmmmm mmmmm mmmmm mmmmm mmmmm mmm mm m... Oh... God.

Pause.

Followed by a longer pause.

WOMAN: 'Ave you finished, then?

Fair Trade

The first off-peak London train of the morning and two elderly northern ladies fall gratefully into their seats. Lady 1 holds out a handful of coins for her friend to take.

LADY 1: Now then, love 'ow much do I owe ye?

LADY 2: Ooh no, love, it dun't matter.

LADY 1: No, go on, love, let me give ye some money!

LADY 2: Nooo, I don't 'ave to pay after half-nine.

LADY 1: No, love, honest, I must pay ye.

LADY 2: No love, honest! Tell ye what, just buy me a cuppa tea...and a nice bun.

LADY 1: I'll buy ye some toast.

LADY 2: Toast?

LADY 1: Aye! Cuppa tea and some toast.

Lady 2 regards Lady 1 disapprovingly as she feeds her handful of coins back into her purse.

LADY 2: Aye, all right then. *Toast.*

Animal Trouble

Friends in a bar have been discussing strange accidents.

YOUNG MAN: My girlfriend's ex, right? Wakes up in hospital
with his head bandaged, concussion, the full works. No idea
how he got there. Over the next couple of days he's in the
hospital and he starts remembering that he'd got up to get a
drink of water from the kitchen. When he got there, he noticed
the sink still had some water in it, so despite the fact he's stark
bollock naked, he decides to go under the sink with a bowl and
drain the water off, yeah? That's the last thing he remembers.
Turns out what happened is his three-month-old kitten has
followed him downstairs and has been watching what's going
on. The bloke bends down to have a go at the sink, right?
Kitten sees these great hairy bollocks hanging down and
decides he's going to give them a bit of a batter. Claws out.
Whallop! Still had one of the little bastard's claws stuck in his
scrote, didn't he?

YETTIE: That's nothing. A friend of mine was working in
Nigeria, and you've got to understand, in Africa, we're a lot
less sentimental about dogs and stuff over there. So when one
dies it just sort of gets left there until another animal drags it
off or something. Anyway, it's hot, and my friend is walking to
work down this strip of grass and he's just passing this dead
dog when, boom! This friend's worked in war zones before,
yeah, so he thinks, shit! Then he realises he feels wet. He's
just about to panic, thinking he's been zapped by a landmine

or something, when he notices the dead dog's gone, yeah. The fucking thing got heated up and exploded all over him. I mean, maggots, shit, bits of stomach, whatever the thing last ate, you know? That was years ago, but still, mention it now and he pukes instantly.